Routledge Revivals

An Essay on India's National Income

First published in 1939, *An Essay on India's National Income: 1925-1929* by V. K. R. V. Rao is a pioneering study of India's economic structure during the late colonial period. The book meticulously examines income sources across agriculture, livestock, forestry, mining, industry, transport and trade employing innovative statistical methods for its time. Rao critiques previous estimates, provides detailed deductions, and offers a comprehensive analysis of national income. A foundational work for economic historians and researchers.

An Essay on India's National Income

1925-1929

V. K. R. V. Rao

Routledge
Taylor & Francis Group
ROUTLEDGE REVIVALS

First published in 1939
by George Allen & Unwin Ltd.

This edition first published in 2026 by Routledge
4 Park Square, Milton Park, Abingdon, Oxon, OX14 4RN

and by Routledge
605 Third Avenue, New York, NY 10158

Routledge is an imprint of the Taylor & Francis Group, an informa business

A Library of Congress record exists under LCCN: 39014375

ISBN: 978-1-041-32608-3 (hbk)
ISBN: 978-1-003-78359-6 (ebk)
ISBN: 978-1-041-32609-0 (pbk)

Book DOI 10.4324/9781003783596

AN ESSAY ON INDIA'S NATIONAL INCOME 1925-1929

by

V. K. R. V. RAO
PH.D. (CANTAB.)
Principal and Professor of Economics
S.L.D. Arts College
Ahmedabad

WITH A PREFACE BY

KRISHNALAL M. JHAVERI
Chairman of the Board of Trustees
Dadabhai Naoroji Memorial Prize Fund

LONDON
GEORGE ALLEN & UNWIN LTD
MUSEUM STREET

FIRST PUBLISHED IN 1939

PRINTED IN GREAT BRITAIN BY
THE ABERDEEN UNIVERSITY PRESS LTD., ABERDEEN

INTRODUCTION

The calculation of India's National Income has always been a subject of absorbing interest to Indian economists; and when the trustees of the Dadabhai Naoroji Memorial Prize Essay Fund invited me to write an essay on this subject in 1933 I readily accepted their invitation, though I knew full well the difficulties attending the task and the comparatively unsatisfactory results it would lead to. I could not take up the writing of the essay till the July of 1934, though I did do some preliminary work in Cambridge side by side with my studies for the Economics Tripos of that University. The essay was completed in February of 1935 and awarded the Dadabhai Naoroji Prize early in the beginning of 1936. It now finds publication in more or less its original form as submitted to the Trustees; and the author hopes it will receive an indulgent criticism from the public.

It is, however, necessary to explain in this preface that the author's researches into Indian Income did not stop with the writing of this essay. In fact, this essay may be said to have begun that research rather than ended it. As will be perceived by those who have the patience to read the following pages, the calculations of the national income embodied therein are based on a study of such official and unofficial data as have been published but not on personal investigation. In a sense, therefore, this study may be said to be a culmination of the type of investigation into Indian Income characteristic of existing publications on the subject, beginning with Dr. Naoroji's and ending with that of Messrs. Shah and Khambhata. But it also revealed to the author, more clearly perhaps than any abstract thinking on the subject would have done, the need for *ad hoc* studies to supplement published data, the desirability of making the calculations for a census year rather than for an inter-censal period, and above all the necessity for calculating the margin of error in the estimates and using care and caution in stating one's statistical results. The author's interest in the subject, thus aroused by the writing of this essay, led him to select India's National Income in the year 1931-32 as the subject for his research for the Ph.D. degree in Economics of the University of Cambridge; and he worked on that subject for 27 months, from June 1934 to August 1937, under the supervision of Mr. Colin Clark, Lecturer in statistics at the University of Cambridge. The author was awarded the Adam Smith Prize in Political Economy by the University of Cambridge in January 1936 on an essay based on the results of this research; in November 1936 he was awarded the Ph.D. degree by the same University. This thesis will be published in due course, and the author would like to point out that these two studies of the Indian Income, one for the period 1925-29 dealt with in this essay and the other for the year 1931-32 dealt with in the author's doctorate thesis, are both independent studies, based on different methods, and, taken together, serve to throw fresh light on the subject of Indian Income.

I am indebted to my friend, Dr. P. M. Joshi, Librarian, University of Bombay, for compiling the Index.

V. K. R. V. RAO.

AHMEDABAD, 11th *Jan.* 1938.

PREFACE

SOON after the death of Dr. Dadabhai Naoroji, a public meeting of the citizens of Bombay was held to mourn his death, and it was decided at that meeting to start a Memorial Fund for the purpose of perpetuating the memory of this distinguished and revered Indian patriot. The proceeds of the Fund were utilised for erecting a Statue; the balance was formed into a Trust Fund known as the Dadabhai Naoroji Memorial Prize Fund for the purpose of a prize to be awarded annually or from time to time to any person who "in the opinion of the Trustees shall have done most to advance the educational, social and economic or other interests of India, or to any person whom the Trustees may select for doing any research work and writing a thesis on any subject connected with the educational, social and economic or other interests of India." Accordingly, the Trustees invited Principal V. K. R. V. Rao to write an Essay on "India's National Income," that Essay is now published by them in book form. The Trustees hope that Dr. Rao's efforts will stimulate further interest in this important subject.

KRISHNALAL M. JHAVERI,
Chairman, Board of Trustees,
Dadabhai Naoroji Memorial Prize Fund.

BOMBAY, *October* 1938.

CONTENTS

Chapter I

PREVIOUS ESTIMATES

A number of estimates of the Indian National Income have been made in the past, and will no doubt be made in the future; for the quest after the elusive figure of the *per capita* income is really a most fascinating field of study, not merely because of the numerous interesting figures one has to gather before one reaches the goal, but also because there is a definiteness and a completeness about the *per capita* income which is not to be seen in the results of other economic investigations. Actually, however, this definiteness is the most misleading characteristic of such a figure, and contributes not a little to the bad reputation which statistics have acquired in common conversation.

Thus, for example, the National Income is made up of the totals of a number of individual money incomes, but the marginal utility of money to the different owners of income is widely different, and the National Income becomes in result a sum of dissimilar units. Then again, what is individual income is not necessarily national income, and what is national income is not necessarily income to the individual. And above all, there is the immense difficulty of obtaining the necessary statistics without which the figure cannot be compiled. In spite of these, and many other considerations, over which we do not enlarge in this work, the concept of national income has come to stay ; and the works of men like Flux, Bowley, Gini, Mitchell, King, Stamp, Sutcliffe and Clark are ample proof of the real importance of trying to compute the country's national income, and in our own country we have had a series of attempts, beginning with Dr. Dadabhai Naoroji's in 1871, and none can say that these attempts are now finally over.

Before proceeding to enter upon our own calculations, it may be worth while to describe and discuss briefly the estimates made so far ; for the best way of avoiding mistakes and overcoming difficulties in any particular branch of knowledge is to study the attempts previously made in that field. We give below a summary statement of the various attempts made so far :—

Author.	Year when attempt was made.	Year for which estimates are made.	Estimates of *per capita* income in Rs.	Territory covered by the attempt.
Dr. Dadabhai Naoroji	1876	1868	20	Br. India
Baring and Barbour .	1882	1882	27	,,
Lord Curzon . .	1901	1897-98	30	,,
William Digby . .	1902	1899	18	,,
F. G. Atkinson . .	1908	1875	27·3	,,
,, . .	,,	1895	35·2	,,
Sir B. N. Sarma .	1921	1911	50	,,
,, ,,	,,	,,	86	,,
Findlay Shirras . .	1922	1921	107	,,
,, ,,	,,	1922	116	,,
Shah and Khambhata	1924	1921	74	Whole of India
Wadia and Joshi .	1925	1913-14	44·3	,,
Vakil and Muranjan .	1926	1925	74	,,
Simon Commission's Report . . .	1929	Not stated	100	,,

In an appendix to this chapter we give details of all these estimates ; out of these, however, we propose to discuss below only the estimates made by Dr. Dadabhai Naoroji for 1871, William Digby for 1899, F. G. Atkinson for 1895, and Shah and Khambhata for 1921, as these are the most elaborate of all the attempts made so far.

Dr. Dadabhai Naoroji's Estimate.

In July 1870 Dr. Naoroji read a paper on " The Wants and Means of India " before the East India Association, wherein he made a rough estimate of the *per capita* income of British India on the basis of land revenue and other revenue figures. He followed it up by trying to work out the problem directly from such official data as he could get from published documents, and his conclusions were embodied in a paper entitled " Poverty of India " which he read in 1876 to the Bombay Branch of the East India Association of London.[1] His results were as on Table overleaf.[2]

As regards his estimates of the quantity and value of agricultural production, Dr. Naoroji's method was at once simple and adequate. He took the figures of the price, yield per acre and area under cultivation of

[1] This interesting footnote accompanies the paper :—

" These notes in their original draft were placed before the Select Committee on Indian Finance in 1873. They were taken, but not published with the Report, as they did not suit the views of the chairman (Mr. Ayrton), and, I was led to suppose, also of Sir Grant Duff, who was then the Under-Secretary of State for India."

[2] The figures exclude the provinces of Sind and Berar ; but this omission does not affect the validity of the *per capita* figure.

the principal crop or crops in each province, and arrived at an average value of the income per acre which he thereupon applied to the total area under cultivation in that province and thus obtained the value of its agricultural produce. From the figure thus obtained, he deducted 10 per cent. in order to make allowance for the fact that the minor or non-principal crop of the provinces were not as valuable as the principal crop and that the prices he used, having been taken from the towns, would presumably be

(In crores of Rs.)
A crore = 10 millions.

Value of agricultural produce . . .	260
„ meat, milk, etc. . . .	15
„ produce of industry . . .	15
„ produce of mines and commerce .	17
Total . .	307
Contingencies .	33
Grand total .	340

Population	170 millions.
Per capita income	Rs. 20

higher than rural prices. It might appear at first sight that Dr. Naoroji would have done better to have taken the area under each crop separately and muliplied it by its yield per acre and price rather than apply to all the cultivated area an average annual value per acre ; but actually his method was less open to error, because in his days there were not detailed figures of classification of the area under cultivation by different crops ; in so far as they were available, they were not as trustworthy as they are to-day.

Further, estimates of yield per acre were not available; in so far as they were available, they were far more reliable for the principal crops than for the minor ones, and the same remark applies with even greater force to statistics of the prices of agricultural produce. Even to-day, e.g., detailed classification of the cultivated area and estimates of yield are available for only 80 per cent. of the total area and we have to take recourse to Dr. Naoroji's method of applying to the remaining area an average value per acre calculated from the value of the agricultural produce of the area for which figures are available.

As a matter of fact, Dr. Naoroji's figures of the value of agricultural produce are as good an estimate as one could possibly get in those days; this is evident when we compare his results with the figures of the quantity and value of agricultural produce in 1876-77 supplied in evidence to the Famine Commission of 1880 by different provincial governments.

The Table on page 14 is based on the replies to the questions 3 and 16 of that Commission's Questionnaire. It will appear that Dr. Naoroji's figures are very much of an under-estimate, as his total is Rs. 74 crores less than that based on the figures of the Famine Commission. But the official figures are not quite a fair account of actual conditions, particularly in the case of North-West Provinces and Madras, for which they appear to be overestimates.

Thus, for example, in the North-West Provinces and Oudh, Mr. Elliot works out figures per district on the data of cultivated areas and yield per acre.

But he does not base his figures of final yield on this data. He assumes that the districts have an export surplus over and above a certain minimum which he regards as reasonable consumption and he makes an addition to his original figures in order to bring them up to this standard. Thus on this score he raised the outturn of food grain from 286 million mds. to 314 millions, of oil seeds from 5 to 20 millions, of the value of vegetables by 50 per cent.; the outturn

Province.	Dr. Naoroji's figures (in lakhs of Rs.).	Figures based on data contained in the evidence before the Famine Commission.
Central Provinces . .	1600	1760
Punjab	3600	2593
North-West Provinces and Oudh . . .	5300	8305
Bengal . . .	9600	12787
Madras . . .	3600	7665
Bombay . . .	4000	2047
Total .	27700	35157

of tobacco is raised from 1·1 to 2·1 million mds. and the total figure is swelled by estimated outputs of milk, ghee, opium, and indigo; the total amount thus allowed for in various ways to bring up the value of the calculated output to the self-sufficiency plus export surplus standard is as much as Rs. 17 crores. To make the figure reasonable and comparable with those of other provinces, it would be necessary to reduce the total for North-West Provinces and Oudh by Rs. 17 crores, thus leaving it at Rs. 66 crores.

The figure for the outturn of food crop of Madras is based on an estimated yield of 1621 lbs. of paddy per acre, while two other estimates given in the same memorandum are of 1200 lbs. and 1000 lbs. No satisfactory explanation is given for the preference of the first estimate of 1621 lbs. As the figure for the value of the entire agricultural produce of Madras is on the basis of this yield, it may be reasonable to reduce this figure by 20 per cent. to make it comparable with the figures of other provinces. The Madras total would then be Rs. 61 crores.

Dr. Naoroji's figure for Bengal is lower than that based on the evidence before the Famine Commission, while his figure for Bombay is higher than that based on the latter. This is due to the fact that the prices used by Dr. Naoroji for his estimating the value of agricultural produce from Bengal are lower than the official prices, while in the case of Bombay, he adopted figures of average yield, which were higher than the official ones. We may therefore adopt the official figures as a more accurate representation of actual conditions. The corrected official total thus comes to Rs. 318 crores. But Dr. Naoroji's figure relates to the year 1867-68, while those of the witnesses before the Famine Commission relate to the year 1877-78, and while the weighted index number of prices was 112 in 1867-68 it was 133 in 1877-78. The price level in 1867-68 seems to be therefore 15 per cent. less than in 1877-78, and in order to make these figures comparable with those of Dr. Naoroji, they will have to be reduced at least by 10 per cent. We do not reduce them by exactly 15 per cent. as price statistics were not quite reliable for purposes of comparison in this period, and a rise in the index number from 95 to 112 simply shows a rise of a fairly substantial character. The official figure, thus corrected by us, would be Rs. 286 crores. But it must further be remembered that the output of agricultural crops would be higher in 1878 than in 1871 as the area under cultivation had increased in the meanwhile, and even if we deduct Rs. 10 crores as value of the increase in output during this period (which represents a rise in output of a little less than 3 per cent. in 10 years, which is not unreasonable) we will get Rs. 276 crores as the finally corrected official figure of the value of agricultural produce of British India in 1867-68, and Dr. Naoroji's figure is Rs. 277 crores. It seems to me that it is a most remarkable tribute to Dr. Naoroji as a statistician that his results should be practically identical with those that are based on all the elaborate data which was available for a Government Commission, and his figure of the value of agricultural produce may therefore be accepted as an authoritative estimate.[1]

[1] We may mention here a criticism advanced against Dr. Naoroji's figure of the value of agricultural production. It was pointed out in a memorandum by Mr. Danvers sent to Dr. Naoroji by Sir Louis Mallet, the then Under-Secretary of State for India, that his calculations made no allowance for straw. In reply, Dr. Naoroji pointed out that he had not only omitted straw, but " also grass, cotton seed and any fodder or other food for animals," on the ground that it would make no difference to the ultimate result. The principle he enunciated is best explained in his own words. " First, either the whole *gross* annual

The really weak points in his thesis are to be found in the estimates of the value of produce from meat, milk, industry, mines and commerce.

No reasons are given for the adoption of the figure of Rs. 15 crores as the value of the output of meat and milk produced in the country; and the figure in question is frankly set down by the author "as a guess only." [1] When it is remembered that in 1875, the earliest year for which figures of cattle census are available, there were 27 million buffaloes and cows, it is obvious that Rs. 15 crores would be an under-estimate even as applied only to their yield of milk; when it is held to include in addition the output of meat and of fish as well, it becomes obvious that there is something wrong with the estimate. As a matter of fact, our own calculations for the quinquennium 1925-29 reveal the value of the output of meat, milk and fish as somewhere in the order of 25 per cent. of the value of agricultural produce; a similar percentage applied to the figures of 1867-68 would give Rs. 65

production of the country may be taken (including straw, grass, etc.) and from this *gross* production, before apportioning it per head of human population, a deduction should be made for the portion required for all the stock; or second, all straw, grass and every production raised for animal food should be left out of the calculation, and only the rest of the production which is and can be turned to human use should be apportioned among the human population." For the whole correspondence see pp. 173-193 "Poverty and Un-British Rule in India."

[1] "For the annual produce of stock, and fish for human consumption, as milk or meat, I can hardly get sufficient data to work upon. I hope Government will give the particulars more fully so that the annual production of stock for consumption, either as milk or meat, may be known. I set it down as £15 millions as a guess only," (p. 24, "Poverty and Un-British Rule in India"). We may add that to this day, Government have not supplied the figures referred to by Dr. Naoroji.

crores as the value of the output of meat, milk and fish and not Rs. 15 crores.[1]

The figure of Rs. 15 crores at which is estimated the value of industry is again open to the same charge of under-estimation. Dr. Naoroji mentions a figure of £4,000,000 (or Rs. 4 crores) as the value of the industrial output of the Punjab, and deducting from it 50 per cent. to cover the value of raw material, he obtains Rs. 2 crores as the net output of industry. He then proceeds, "The manufactures of other parts of India are not quite so valuable, therefore for the population of all British India, which is about ten times that of the Punjab, if I take £15,000,000 for the value of manufacturing industry, I shall not be far off the mark." The results are simply not credible. It is hardly possible that the value of industrial output should be less than 6 per cent. of the value of agricultural output, when the percentage of the number of people supported by industry alone was 25 per cent. of that supported by agriculture. Indeed one would expect that the value of net output per head of industrial workers would be greater than that of those employed in agriculture. Even if we believe that the relation between the value of agricultural and industrial production in 1867-68 was of the same order as in 1925-29 (in fact, a larger percentage of the total population subsisted on non-agricultural occupations in those days), then the value of industrial output

[1] This figure is based on the assumption (which does not appear to be unreasonable) that livestock held the same position in India's agricultural economy in 1867-68 as it did in post-war times.

would be about Rs. 60 crores as against Dr. Naoroji's figure of Rs. 15 crores.

The output from mines and commerce is valued at Rs. 17 crores. Explanations are offered as to how the profits of commerce have been worked out, but the figure appears reasonable in relation to the magnitude of the other constituents of our national income.

Finally, Dr. Naoroji made no allowance for the contribution to national income made by items such as transport, public force and administration, professions and domestic servants. This was forcibly pointed out by Mr. Danvers (to whose memorandum we have already referred in a footnote on p. 16) in the following words: "Mr. Dadabhai has adopted the principle of equally apportioning the value of agricultural produce and manufactures, as ascertained by him from the statistics available, amongst the whole population, without distinguishing how many are agriculturists, how many mechanics, and how many belong to other trades or professions, or possess property, and whose incomes therefore are derived directly neither from agriculture nor from manufactures. Thus he omits all reference to railway wealth, Government stock, house property, profits of trade, salaries, pensions, non-agricultural wages, professional incomes and returns to investments, and all other sources from which a man who does not grow food himself may obtain the means of purchasing it." Dr. Naoroji made an even more forcible reply, parts of which are worth quoting as illustrating the similar attitude taken up by several subsequent writers on the subject, like Digby and Messrs Shah and Khambhata. " By the mere fact of the removal of the wheat from the Punjab to Bombay, not a single grain of wheat nor a single pie of money is added to what already existed in India before the wheat was touched . . . If the mere movement of produce can *add* to the existing wealth, India can become rich in no time; all it would have to do is to go on moving its produce continually all over India all the year round, and under the magic wheels of the train wealth will go on springing till the land will not suffice to hold it . . . Government stock does not from itself produce or create or make to grow out any money, food, or any kind of material wealth for me . . . The house (*re* house property) does not grow or create the rent by the mere fact of my occupying it . . . Not a single atom of money or wheat is added to the existing wealth of the country by this internal trade, only a different distribution has taken place . . . Official salaries and pensions are paid by Government from revenue and this revenue is derived from the production of the country ; and so from that same source are all such salaries and pensions derived . . . The mere act of my consulting professional gentlemen (e.g. doctors and lawyers) does not enable me to create money to pay them . . . In short, every labourer, mental or physical, has his share for subsistence, through various channels, from the only one fountain head, the annual material production of the country. There is no source outside the production (including any addition to it from profits of foreign trade) from which any individual derives his means of subsistence." [1]

Both criticism and answer are not wholly free from fault. Mr. Danvers was confusing the concept of individual with that of national income when he counted the income from Government stock as an item of the national income; and Dr. Naoroji was quite properly entitled to omit those items. On the other hand, Dr. Naoroji's treatment of the income from transport, domestic service, professions and public administration is clearly based on the old physiocratic concept of the *materiality* of income. In fact, even to-day there are some economists who take up that point of view. While there is no doubt that calculation of the strictly material part of the national income of a country is useful for many purposes, it is admitted now by the majority of economists that income consists of utility and that material goods are items of wealth only in so far as they furnish utility; therefore, services which contain utility would be quite as much income as material goods that contain utility. The point appears quite obvious if we compare the economic condition of two countries each with the same quantity of agricultural and industrial output, but one having lawyers, doctors, domestic servants and transport facilities, the other without any of these. The latter country would be poorer and its comparative poverty would soon take a material form by way of exports of goods to pay for the services it would have to obtain from foreign doctors, lawyers, domestic

[1] "Poverty and Un-British Rule in India," pp. 180-185.

servants, and owners of transport systems. There is no doubt, therefore, that in omitting the value of services from his figure Dr. Naoroji seriously impaired the utility of his estimate. But, on the other hand, we find Dr. Naoroji adding Rs. 33 crores under the head "contingencies" (an amount greater than the combined total of his estimates of the value of the output of meat, milk, fish and of the value of industrial output). We can reasonably regard this item as meant to take the place of the valuation of services; even then the figure appears to be somewhat of an underestimate and may therefore be raised to Rs. 40 crores as the value of the combined services of transport, professions, administration and domestic servants.[1]

We conclude therefore that, altogether, Dr. Naoroji's estimate of our *per capita* income in 1867-68 was an underestimate of the real position, and that, taking into account the corrections we have made and deductions on account of seed, depreciation, etc., the *per capita* income during that year would be more in the region of Rs. 23-24 than in that of Rs. 20; an analysis of his work has also revealed to us the need for care in estimating the value of non-agricultural output.

[1] The census figures for 1875 give 30 millions as supported by industry; and 18 millions as supported by Professions, Transport, etc.; in addition, there were 16 millions who were returned as dependent on labour. If we assign these 16 millions in equal proportions between industry and the rest, we would get 38 millions for Industry and 28 for the rest. Proceeding on our valuation of Rs. 60 crores for industrial output, that should give us a little more than Rs. 40 crores as the value of the output of Professions, Public Administration, Domestic Service and Transport.

William Digby's Estimate.

William Digby's estimate is contained in his "Prosperous British India," a famous and well-documented indictment of the economics of British rule in India, and his figures are a reply to the thesis advanced by Lord Curzon in his speech to the Imperial Legislative Council in March 1901.

Replying to the charge of India's growing poverty under British rule, Lord Curzon pointed out that the agricultural income of India had been estimated by the Famine Commission of 1898 at Rs. 450 crores; assuming that the non-agricultural income of India had increased in the same proportion as the agricultural (i.e. assuming that it is half of the total agricultural income of the country as it was supposed to be by Baring and Barbour in 1882), the total income of India would be Rs. 675 crores, and allowing for the increase in population, His Excellency estimated the *per capita* income of an Indian at Rs. 30 a year—an increase of 11 per cent. from Rs. 27 in 1880, surely a mark of progress!

Digby's book is a very elaborate study of the facts relating to the national income of India. There are several chapters on allied topics, such as the "drain," famines, etc., but the main object of the book is to discover our *per capita* income, and his final conclusions are contained in Chapter XII, entitled "The Present Economic Condition of India—The Declining Income of the Indian People." In this chapter, which covers quite 200 pages, Digby computes the income of India, agricultural and non-agricultural and province by province. He then attempts to discover the share in the national income which goes to the richer classes and finally arrives at what is the *per capita* income of the *masses* in India. His figures are as under :—

	(In millions of £)
Agricultural income . . .	174·8
Non-agricultural income . .	84·8
Total . .	259·6

Population . .	226·5 millions
Per capita income .	£1·15 or Rs. 17·2

Details by provinces, as well as details of his valuation of industrial output are given in the Appendix.

The first thing that strikes us about Digby's figures is that they are considerably lower than Lord Curzon's. As a matter of fact, his estimate of India's agricultural income is lower than even that made by Dr. Naoroji ; in terms of rupees, Digby would place the value of India's agricultural produce in 1899 at Rs. 262 crores, as compared with the Rs. 277 crores of Dr. Naoroji for 1867-68, though within the three intervening decades, the area under cultivation had recorded a considerable increase, irrigation had been extended, and prices of agricultural produce had shown a steady rise. It is inconceivable, therefore, that the absolute value of our agricultural produce should show a fall as compared with 30 years before. The reason for the large difference between Digby's figures of the value of India's agricultural production and those of all the other writers on the subject is quite simple. All the writers on India's national income, with the exception of Digby, took statistics of area under cultivation, area under different crops and yield per acre and multiplied the quantities of output thus arrived at by their prices ; Digby, on the other hand, deliberately rejected this method on the ground that the money value of crops is not accurately ascertainable in India. "I have, consequently, had to adopt another mode. The Government revenue is intended to bear a definite ratio to the assumed (or ascertained) produce of the soil reckoned over a number of years. That ratio differs in the respective presidencies and provinces. It is approximately ascertainable and I have ascertained it as nearly as may be. Possessing it, to arrive at the money value, I have multiplied the land revenue the necessary number of times and have thus reached the result I announce." [1]

The proportions which he used corresponded with those mentioned in Dutt's open letter to Lord Curzon, and are as under :—

In Bengal	5 to 6 per cent.
,, the North-West Province .	8 per cent.
,, Punjab	10 per cent.
,, Madras	12 to 31—say 20 per cent.
,, Bombay	20 to 33— ,, 25 per cent.

There are several objections to this method ; first of all, the basis of land revenue assessment differs from province to province even in the temporary-settled areas, and the figures of the proportion of land revenue demand to the gross value of agricultural produce are, if anything, of even more doubtful validity than

[1] "Prosperous British India," pp. 531-532.

statistics of area, yield and prices. Secondly, quite a large portion of the cultivated area is under permanent settlement, and settlement reports can therefore show no connection between the gross value of agricultural produce and the land revenue assessed on that area. Thirdly, land revenue settlement is usually for a period varying from 20 to 30 years and in any period when prices are moving in either direction, land revenue assessment ceases to be an indicator of the *value* of agricultural produce. Finally, there are special rules of land revenue assessment for areas brought newly under cultivation and for areas which under new settlement show enhanced productivity, with the result that the proportion between land revenue demand and the agricultural income of these areas is not comparable with the similar figure for the remaining area under cultivation. Taking into account all these considerations, we cannot accept this method as *the proper method* for evaluating the agricultural income of British India, and we cannot therefore accept Digby's figure ; at the same time, there is no doubt that Digby's method can be used as a useful supplement to check the figures of the value of agricultural production arrived at on the direct method ; and from that point of view Digby's figures are worth studying.[1]

[1] We may in passing notice a criticism of Digby's method which is not easily understandable. We are told by Messrs. Shah and Khambhata that the method adopted by Digby for agricultural income is untrustworthy and also involves a *petitio principii* ; it tries to find out the gross produce from the multiplier which itself can only be obtained from the gross produce. The result will depend upon which multiplier we select (" Wealth and Taxable Capacity of India, pp. 66-67). The authors imply that the proportions selected by Dutt are arrived

It is not apparent from Digby's book how exactly he arrived at his figures of the value of industrial output. It is true that he gives detailed valuations of 72 items of industrial output from which we may notice a few items such as liquor (£20 millions), clothing (£13·5 millions), hides and skins (£5 millions) and sundries (£13·6 millions) ; but no explanation is offered for the way in which the values of the different items have been calculated except those of clothing and the increase in livestock. At any rate, here is at least an attempt made directly to evaluate industrial output instead of assuming, as was done by Baring and Barbour and Curzon, that non-agricultural income is half of agricultural income, and his figure of Rs. 127 crores is nearer the mark than his estimate of agricultural income. But it must be noted that Digby fails to include in his calculations any amount for the output of services such as professions, government and domestic servants. The omission is deliberate and his figures contain in consequence a further element of underestimation. It therefore seems clear that Digby's figure is almost certainly an underestimate

at by calculating the total value of the agricultural produce and dividing it by the land revenue assessed on the area. Surely neither Dutt nor Digby deserve such a charge. There is such a thing as sampling. And if the assumption is made that there is some uniformity of principle behind land revenue assessment, then collection by sampling of the actual proportion of land revenue demand to gross value of agricultural produce would be the best way of evaluating the gross agricultural income of India. The real criticism against Digby's method lies in his assumption of uniformity and comparability of different provincial land revenue settlements and in his ignoring the effects of changes in area, prices, etc., which take place during the settlement period rather than on the utility of the assessment figure as an indicator of gross agricultural income.

and cannot be accepted as a true picture of Indian conditions in 1899.

F. J. Atkinson's Estimate.

Digby's elaborate criticism of Lord Curzon's figures and his substitution for the latter's figure of one that was just a little more than its half could not obviously pass unchallenged, and challenged they were in a most elaborate and skilfully drafted paper running over more than 60 pages on "A Statistical Review of the Income and Wealth of British India," read before the Royal Statistical Society in the author's absence in June 1902. The author, Mr. Fred. J. Atkinson, was an important official of the Government of India and could claim knowledge of Indian conditions and first hand experience of Indian statistical data. He not merely replied to Mr. Digby's criticism of Lord Curzon's estimates, but proceeded to make fresh estimates on his own of the Indian national income for the years 1875 and 1895,[1] and his figures need to be studied in any history of the estimates of our national income.

Atkinson's study is, in my opinion, notable not so much for the accuracy of his figures—as a matter of fact, they tend to the opposite extreme of overestimation as compared with Digby's—as for the method

[1] We may notice his reply to Digby. Digby had pointed out that whereas Lord Curzon talked of a total cultivated area of 194 million acres for 1880 as against 217 million acres for 1897-98, the statistics furnished by the Director-General showed 183 and 196 million acres respectively for the two years. Atkinson pointed out that Curzon had very properly included in his figures an allowance for the area that bore more than one crop.

which he followed in his calculations and which is explained at length in his paper.

He divided the total earners or working population of the country into two broad classes. First, there was the class supported by agriculture, then there were those subsisting on non-agricultural occupations such as industry, commerce, public administration, domestic service, etc., and the latter class he subdivided into two sections, section II those who were well to do, comprising the richer bankers and merchants, the highly paid civil and military officials and the professional classes, and, section III, consisting of all workers in industry, transport and commerce, the low-paid government servants and those whose occupations were not returned or were of a miscellaneous kind. As regards the first class, he followed the method of calculating the total value of agricultural production by using statistics of area, yield and prices, and the total agricultural income thus obtained was shared among the population subsisting on agriculture. As regards the classes dependent on non-agricultural occupations, there were no similar figures of production which could be used for calculating their income. Atkinson, therefore, conceived the idea of obtaining their total income by getting representative figures of the wages of the different occupational groups and multiplying them by the numbers returned as employed under each group. Where he could not get wage figures for each group, he divided the numbers of employed under that group roughly into "skilled" and "unskilled" and applied to them the wage-rates of skilled and unskilled workers respectively that he had obtained from official sources. Figures of income for the classes under section II, i.e. the well-to-do non-agricultural classes, he obtained from the civil estimates for Government officials and from income tax returns for members of the professional classes. His results are summed up below :—

CLASSIFICATION OF POPULATION

(In millions)

	Male Adults.[1]		Others.		Total.	
	1875.	1895.	1875.	1895.	1875.	1895.
Section I (Agricultural) . .	35·9	42·6	82·5	97·0	118·4	139·6
Section II (Non - agricultural, poorer) . .	20·2	23·5	44·9	53·4	65·1	76·9
Section III (Non - agricultural, well-to-do) . .	1·4	1·7	3·1	3·7	4·5	5·4

INCOME

(In crores of Rs.)

	1875.	1895.
Section I . . .	312·9	501·5
,, II . . .	187·2	262·1
,, III . .	74·0	113·0
Total .	574·1	876·6
Population . . .	18·8	22·2
Per capita income .	Rs. 30·5 in 1875	
	Rs. 39·5 in 1895	

[1] A male adult is defined by him as of age 15 and above.

While Atkinson's method is certainly an improvement on that of his predecessors in the field, his figures are not free from objection. His figure of agricultural income is based on (1) an increased estimate of yield per acre in 1895 as compared with 1875; (2) a rise in prices of 30 per cent. for food crops (as compared with 1875) and 31 per cent. for all crops. Both these assumptions are open to attack.

Atkinson puts the yield per acre in 1895 at *753* lbs. as compared with *724* lbs. in 1875. The increase in yield is attributed to extension of irrigation, and improvement in the art of cultivation. The latter assumption is of doubtful validity; on the other hand, deforestation and the growing use of cow dung as fuel were impairing the productive capacity of the soil. As regards the improvement in the general average yield per acre attributed to irrigation, it must be remembered that Atkinson's own figure of 724 lbs. for 1875 is a composite average that takes the increased yield on irrigated land into account as the yield per acre on unirrigated land was only 553 lbs. Under the circumstances, mere extension of the area under irrigation is no reason for increasing the average yield per acre unless the increase has been of such dimensions as to increase the proportion of the area under irrigation to the total cultivated area from what it was in 1875. This is not shown by Atkinson; we must therefore conclude that the agricultural output which Atkinson assigns to 1895 contains a substantial amount of overestimation (the increase in yield arising from improved agricultural efficiency as calculated by Atkinson was as much as 54·5 million cwts.).

Then again, we are not able to see how Atkinson arrives at his figure of 31 per cent. as the increase in the price of all crops in 1895 as compared with 1875.[1] A reference to the Index Number of Indian Prices gives the following result :—

(1873 = 100)

	Exported articles (unweighted).	Imported articles (unweighted).	General Index No. for all (unweighted).	Weighted Index No.
1875 . .	95	90	94	96
1895 . .	111	87	104	120

The increase in prices, if one takes the unweighted index numbers of exported articles, is only 17 per cent.; if we take the weighted index number, even then the increase is only 25 per cent. as against the 31 per cent. assumed by Atkinson in his calculations. And a 6 per cent. difference in the average price of all crops will make for a difference of as much as Rs. 30 crores in the totals of the value of agricultural produce. Moreover, Atkinson has made no allowance for seed and wastage, nor, so far as one can see, has any allowance been made for depreciation under any of the heads of income. Following the practice of the Famine Commission, we may deduct 10 per cent. from his figure of agricultural income for seed, wastage and depreciation, while 5 per cent. would be a very moderate

[1] His statement on the subject is not very illuminating. "The average price of each crop has been carefully worked out from the various returns, etc., and may be accepted as approximately correct. Prices were 30 per cent. higher in 1895 than in 1875 for food crops and 31 per cent. for all crops." *Ibid.*, p. 218.

allowance for depreciation on non-agricultural income (excluding professions and public administration, for which no allowance for depreciation need be made). Atkinson's figure of the value of Indian agricultural output is therefore undoubtedly an overestimate (even as Digby's was an underestimate).

Even his figures of the value of the income attributed to those who were engaged in non-agricultural occupations contains large elements of error. The crucial figure in his calculations, viz. the number of earners in non-agricultural occupations, is assumed to be equal to all the males of the ages of 15 and above returned as supported by the occupation in question, and they are supposed to be continually employed, but he adds that he has not taken into account the large number of women and children under 15 who are also earners, and therefore it is sufficient if he deducted 5 per cent. from his totals of non-agricultural income on this account. We suggest that the deduction allowed is not adequate to meet the facts of the situation. It is true that he has not taken into account the number of women who are also earners, but these are not considerable in number, while as against this it must be remembered that all males of 15 and above are not necessarily earners. A number of them below 20 and almost all of them above 60 must be dependents; in addition a part of the male adult population will be incapable of work, due to physical ailments. If these two sets of figures are set off against each other, then lack of continued employment has to be allowed for. Atkinson's deduction on this account is 5 per cent., while even if we assume that non-agricultural workers are gainfully employed for 310 days in the year, the deduction to be made is 15 per cent., and this would mean that Atkinson's figures of the income under section II has to be reduced by Rs. 20 crores for 1875 and Rs. 28 crores for 1895—considerable deductions. Then again, in the details of his calculations, Atkinson commits certain curious errors. Thus he includes 8·5 lakhs of *mendicants* for 1875 in his category of earners and at a rate of Rs. 62·8 per year per head he values their contribution to the national income at Rs. 5·3 crores; the corresponding figures for 1895 are 9·8 lakhs mendicants, average income per head Rs. 72·6 per year, annual contribution to national income, Rs. 7·1 crores; Obviously, it is ridiculous to include beggars as positive contributors to the national dividend; even the census occupational tables class them as "unproductive class," and Rs. 5 and Rs. 7 crores must accordingly be deducted from Atkinson's totals under section II for 1875 and 1895. Then again, under section III are included for 1895 Rs. 52 crores as the incomes of the well-to-do classes engaged in commerce. Under the same head there have already been included Rs. 6·2 crores in section II. Moreover, the prices which have been used to evaluate agricultural output are wholesale prices and presumably include at least a part of the profits of commerce. On these grounds, we will be justified in reducing the Rs. 52 crores by 50 per cent., i.e. by Rs. 26 crores. Moreover, Atkinson has included Rs. 10·7 crores as "Private Incomes"; this consists of the incomes of holders of Government securities and other rentiers; surely these incomes form a claim on the national income, not an addition to it, and they ought to be omitted from any proper computation of the national income.

It is very difficult to go into the details of his other figures as sufficient data is not available, but I believe enough has been said to show that Mr. Atkinson's figures are *undeniably an overestimate.* If we make the deductions we have found necessary, his figure of the national income for 1895 as corrected by us would be as follows : [1]—

[1] The deductions are as under :—

Under Section I—

Crores.	
Rs. 30·1,	against overestimate in increase in prices.
Rs. 18·9,	against overestimate in increase in output.
Rs. 45·2,	for seed, wastage and depreciation.
Rs. 94·2	(Total).

Under Section II—

Crores.	
Rs. 28,	against overestimate in number of days employed of workers.
Rs. 7·1,	against incomes of beggars.
Rs. 7·8,	for depreciation.
42·9	(Total).

Under Section III—

Crores.	
Rs. 26,	against double counting of income from commerce.
Rs. 10·7,	against incomes of those living on " Private Income."
36·7	(Total).

	Atkinson's figure.	Atkinson's figure as corrected by us.
	(In crores of Rs.).	
Section I . .	501·5	407·3
„ II . .	262·1	219·2
„ III . .	113·0	76·3
Total . . .	876·6	702·8

Population . . 22·2 crores
Per capita income . Rs. 39·5—Atkinson's.
31·5—Corrected.

Atkinson's figure as amended would give Rs. 31·5 per year as the *per capita* income as against Rs. 23·5 for 1867-68 which is Dr. Naoroji's figure as amended, and if we allow for the rise in prices which had taken place in the meanwhile, we find that the *corrected* figure of Atkinson is quite a reasonable statement of economic conditions in 1895; his original figures however contain undoubted elements of exaggeration and tend to present too rosy a picture of India's economic position in that year.

Shah and Khambhata's Estimate.

The next really elaborate study of the national income was by Messrs. Shah and Khambhata in their "Wealth and Taxable Capacity of India," published in 1924. This work can really be described as the first thorough and comprehensive discussion of the problems connected with India's national income, and in many respects their results marked an advance on the works of previous investigators. The results of their investigations are summed up in the following table :—

	(Figures in crores of Rs.).			
	1900-14.	1914-22.	1900-22.	1921-22.
Net agricultural production (i.e. deduction for seeds) . . .	994·8	1651·5	1232·1	2097·8
Forests . . .	10·0	20·0	14·0	28·0
Fisheries . . .	1·2	2·5	1·9	3·2
Manufactures . .	80·0	150·0	106·0	186·0
Minerals . . .	10·0	21·6	14·0	28·7
Building, etc. . .	10·0	16·4	12·0	20·3
Total .	1160·0	1862·0	1380·0	2364·0
Per capita income in Rs.	36	58½	44½	74

The income from cattle is treated as nil, as the value of hides, skins, bones, horns, manure, meat, milk, accretions to livestock, etc., are taken to be off-set by the cost of upkeep of the animals, so as to leave income nil.

There are several criticisms which immediately suggest themselves in the light of our discussions of previous estimates.

The value of non-agricultural income is very small as compared with that of agricultural income. In fact, non-agricultural income in 1921 would be placed by the authors at less than 1/9th of agricultural income though the population subsisting on non-agricultural occupations was more than 1/3rd of that subsisting on agriculture ; the incongruity becomes more evident when we remember that normally an industrial worker earns more than an agricultural worker. It seems obvious that the figure of Rs. 74 for 1921 must be an underestimate.

The explanation is to be found in certain theoretical opinions held by the authors regarding what ought and what ought not to be included in the national income. Messrs. Shah and Khambhata follow the line taken up by Dr. Naoroji and William Digby in holding that services ought not to be included in a computation of the national dividend. In an interesting chapter on the "Problem of the Inclusion of 'Services' in a Computation of the National Income," the authors try to advance very subtle arguments for the position they have taken up. They suggest that they are talking of "real income" as against the "nominal income" which "would be the sum of commodities and services not resulting in material commodities."[1] Alternatively they would like to "oppose" the term *national dividend* to the term *national income*, i.e. to confine the term *national dividend* to denote the commodity income only, while the term *national income* may be used to denote the sum total of "earnings" or "comings in" from all directions, whether in the shape of material commodities, or in the shape of mere abstract services. The controversy is really endless, and we have already pointed out our views on the subject when discussing Dr. Naoroji's figures. The material point for us to note here is that on account of this predilection of the authors in

[1] "Wealth and Taxable Capacity of India," p. 29.

favour of *material income*, large groups of services such as Public Administration, the Professions and Domestic Services with substantial earnings are excluded from the figure of national income, and to that extent their figures are a substantial underestimate of the national income of India for the year 1921-22 and for the other periods for which they have made their calculations. On the assumption that classes employed in Professions, Public Administration and Domestic Service bore in 1921 the same relation in our national economy to those engaged in Agriculture as they did in 1925-29—which is a reasonable enough assumption—the total income attributable to those classes and omitted by the authors is Rs. 173 crores. This will have to be added to their figures if they are to be made comparable with those of Naoroji and Atkinson as amended by us.

As regards commercial and transport services, the authors are prepared to waive the objection that they are not material utilities, and are willing to include these services in a computation of material wealth. Even this admission, however, is accompanied by a curious qualification—which really pertains more to the ethics of distribution rather than a calculation of total income—that this inclusion " must only be to the extent of those added utilities, and not the whole amount of the big profits or profiteering that may have been made." In practice, we find them making no addition whatsoever to the national income against the value of transport and commercial services. We are told that as the prices they have taken are wholesale prices, they include transport and commercial services, and that in so far as retail services are left out the value of their income is offset by the fact that valuation at wholesale prices is applied to the entire agricultural produce and not merely to the portion that is actually sold for money. The first point appears sound in theory, but when one knows the extent of rational connection that exists between records of harvest and of wholesale prices in India, it is apparent that some separate allowance has still to be made for the value of transport services. Regarding the second assumption, viz. that the value of retail services is exactly offset by the application of wholesale prices to that part of agricultural produce which is not sold for cash, I am not able to make any comments, as the authors do not give any reasons for their attitude. But the argument that their figure is an underestimate is considerably strengthened by these omissions. It is difficult to estimate the monetary value of the figure thus omitted by them, but if we calculate on the basis that the incomes of half the population under the census head " Trade and Transport " are omitted from their estimate, the other half having been accounted for by the application of wholesale prices to agricultural produce, and that the *per capita* income of members of this class was the same as that of those dependent on agriculture—figures for the latter being taken from the calculations of Shah and Khambhata themselves—then we get Rs. 98 crores as the value of the items excluded by Shah and Khambhata, and this Rs. 98 crores should therefore be added to their figures in order to make it comparable with the corrected figures of previous estimates.

In this connection, their treatment of the income from cattle may also be noticed. They point out that the total income from cattle is Rs. 235 crores, while the cost of their upkeep is calculated at Rs. 228 crores, with the result that there is practically no net income from cattle.[1] The value of the annual production of milk as estimated by them is unduly low. Only half the total number of cows and cow-buffaloes are considered to be milkers; these again are supposed to give milk only for six months in the year at the rate of 3 lbs. per day. And the price of milk in the year 1921-22 is assumed to be *one anna per seer.* I believe that there is a mistake in the table by which lb. and seer are treated as identical; even then, their price would work out at as. 2 a seer or 8 seers per rupee, which surely is an underestimate of the actual price of milk during that year. There is no doubt that Messrs. Shah and Khambhata's estimate of the annual value of milk production is an underestimate of the actual position.

If we allow the price of milk to be 6 seers per rupee, the corrected figure for milk and milk products would be Rs. *173* crores, and, therefore, Rs. 43 crores will

[1] Details are as under (for the year 1920-21) :—

Hides and skins	Rs. 18	crores.
Bones, horns, etc. . . .	Rs. 2	,,
Manure	Rs. 45	,,
Meat	Rs. 32	,,
Milk and milk products . .	Rs. 130	,,
Accretions to cattle and horses .	Rs. 8	,,
	——	,,
Total .	Rs. 235	,,
Cost of upkeep	Rs. 228	,,

have to be added to their figures as the *net* yield of livestock.

Then again, Rs. 40 crores is assigned as the value of the net output of wealth from handicrafts which include "handweaving, dying, calico printing, metal working, silkweaving and sericulture, wood carving, lacquer working, pottery and other artistic industries like ivory carving and inlaying, etc." [1] Surely this is an underestimate of the earnings of a section of the population, who are several times the number of those engaged in factory industries and whose total income is estimated at Rs. 146 crores. It is, of course, true that the income of those engaged in producing goods on a large scale and with the help of machinery would be much greater per head than that of those engaged in handicrafts, as the former will include a substantial amount for the profits of capital. Of the 33 millions dependent on industry (1921 census), on a liberal estimate 8 millions may be dependent on large scale industry; the remaining 25 millions may be assigned to handicrafts. That we are, if at all, only erring on the safe side is shown by the fact that Messrs. Shah and Khambhata admit about handweaving alone that all over India it is the sole occupation of over half a crore of people, and if the proportion of the number of workers to total population supported by the occupation is one third, then this alone would account for 15 millions; while for the remaining 10 millions, there have to be taken into account metal working, wood carving, pottery, smithing, carpentry and other

[1] "Wealth and Taxable Capacity of India," p. 187.

items of handicrafts. If we assume further that the average income of a person dependent on handicraft is one third that of one engaged in large scale industry, then the total income due to handicrafts ought to be Rs. 152 crores. This is a conservative estimate, as our figures give a larger proportion of dependents to workers for large-scale industry than we give for handicrafts. As Shah and Khambhata have only allowed Rs. 40 crores under the head, we have to add to their figure the remaining 112 crores of Rs.

We summarise below Messrs. Shah and Khambhata's figures as corrected by us :—

	(Crores of Rs.)
Shah and Khambhata's figure	2364
Add under profession, public administration and domestic service	173
Add under transport and trade	98
Add for livestock	43
Add under manufactures, handicrafts	112
Grand total	2790
Population	31·6 crores.
Per capita income (as amended)	Rs. 88
As per Shah and Khambhata	Rs. 74

We see, therefore, that the estimate of Rs. 74 made by Messrs. Shah and Khambhata of our *per capita* income in 1921-22 contains a considerable element of understatement and should be increased by Rs. 14 or very nearly 19 per cent.

Conclusion.

We have now surveyed the most important of the numerous estimates which have been made till now of our national income. It only remains for us to draw from this study certain guiding principles which will determine our own calculations of national income.

(1) It is desirable to apply the method of an average value per acre to the area for which authoritative details of crop yields and of prices are not available rather than try to get from out-of-date and inefficient sources estimates of their area, yield and price and thus multiply error by error (Dr. Naoroji).

(2) It is necessary to pay particular attention to non-agricultural sources of income, and in this connection the method of classification of earners into occupational groups and calculation of their income through the application of the average wage rates of those groups is worth adopting (Atkinson and Shirras).

(3) Income from livestock needs particular study, as available official statistics are very meagre (Dr. Naoroji).

(4) Quantity and price figures for a year are open to considerable objection: it is better to calculate the national income for a period of years (Shah and Khambhata).

(5) Need for carefully calculating the necessary deductions in the shape of seed, wastage, raw materials imported from abroad, depreciation, etc.

Above all, our study has revealed a number of pitfalls into which even the most experienced investigator into the national income is apt to fall; and we shall therefore undertake our study with the humility and the fear that the subject should command.

In the next chapter we discuss the available statistical data and the method we intend to follow in the light of our studies of previous estimates as well as of existing data. We shall then enter into a discussion of the number of incomes in the country and their distribution over different occupations. We shall then take up different sources of national income and discuss their output and the value of their output for the quinquennium 1925-29. We shall begin with agriculture and go on in serial order with livestock, forests, minerals, manufactures, transport, trade, public administration, professions and liberal arts, and domestic servants. In the eleventh chapter we shall discuss deductions to be made from the gross income in order to arrive at the consumable (not actually consumed, for a part of our income may be and is saved) income. In a final chapter, we shall sum up our results and arrive at an estimate of the annual *per capita* income of India on the basis of our statistics for the quinquennium 1925-29.

Chapter II

STATISTICS AND METHOD

When we come to discuss the method to be employed in calculating the Indian National Dividend we are faced with a lamentable dearth of statistical material. The usual methods employed in calculating the national dividend in other countries, viz. those resting on the use of income tax statistics and of the census of production, cannot be employed in our country. The Indian income tax is restricted to non-agricultural incomes and in a country where more than 70 per cent. of the population are directly dependent on agriculture, the seriousness of the omission needs no emphasis. The income tax figures furnish no evidence of the magnitude of even the non-agricultural income, for, with the minimum taxable income at Rs. 2000, there were hardly more than three lakhs of assessees. There is no census of production in our country. There are great difficulties in the way of a census of agricultural production in any country, and in the absence of literacy and intelligence on the part of the rural population to submit returns of income, it is almost impossible to get a direct estimate of agricultural production. The Government of India issues annual statements of cropped area, areas under different crops, and the statistics of yield for the important crops. There is no census of industrial production. A so-called industrial census was carried out in 1921, but it contains no figures of output, and the experiment was not repeated in 1931. Recently, however, the Government of India has begun issuing a monthly survey of business conditions in India which gives figures of output for selected organised industries. Even the income tax statistics do not give details for the important sources of income, though these are available for the years before 1920. There is a fairly complete account of mineral production. The Government of India issue no statistics of wages since the discontinuance of "Prices and Wages in India" in 1922. The Punjab, the Central Provinces and the Madras Governments appear to have a quinquennial wage-census, but there are no similar publications for the other provinces, with the exception of an enquiry into agricultural wages in the Bombay presidency. Some indication of numbers, if not of wages, is contained in the occupational statistics contained in the decennial census reports. We may now make a brief analysis of the statistics available for computing income under each of the principal sources of the national dividend.

Agriculture.

This of course is the most important head, and we have figures of area and yield for the more important crops.[1] The statistics of yield are computed on the basis of the following formula :—

> Standard yield × State of the crop for the year expressed in terms of a percentage of the standard yield × Cultivated area under that particular crop.

The standard yield is computed on the basis originally of figures compiled for the Famine Commission and then kept up-to-date by crop-cutting experiments in selected Government farms, and it is supposed to represent what the yield would be if all conditions are normal. The " state of the crop " or the anna valuation is made from year to year and is based on the judgments of the state of the crop which village revenue officials entertain. There is undoubtedly room for error in this method, but there is no other way of ascertaining the total quantity of agricultural production, and long experience has no doubt tended to give the village officials' estimate more authority than that of a mere guesswork, while individual errors will probably cancel themelvess when considered for the country as a whole.[2]

As for statistics of prices, three different sets of

[1] Statistics of yield are available both by provinces and for the country as a whole, for the following crops : Rice, wheat, sugarcane, tea, cotton, jute, groundnut, rape and mustard, linseed, seasamum, castor seed, indigo, coffee, rubber, barley, jowar, bajra, maize, gram, and tobacco. These cover very nearly 80 per cent. of the total gross area under crops.

[2] One would have felt more confidence in the figures, however, if a sample census of agricultural production had been carried out at random in a few places and the results used to check up the estimates of output arrived at on the basis of the formula already mentioned.

figures are available which are not all alternative to each other, and they have all been used in valuing our agricultural production. There are the figures of harvest prices given in the provincial Season and Crop reports, and reproduced in the "Agricultural Statistics of India," Vol. I; there are also the figures of wholesale prices [1] for the more important agricultural commodities (mostly those that figure in our exports), in the "Index Number of Indian Prices"; and finally, we get the declared value per unit of exported articles in the "Review of the Trade of India." Of these the first should (if it was properly compiled) represent the value as the cultivator sees it, and the last should be the least faithful reflection of average values. In our calculations we have used, as far as they are available, statistics of harvest prices supplemented where necessary by figures of wholesale prices, failing which the declared value per unit of exported articles has been employed.

The statistics have been worked out separately for each province, as there is a considerable difference in both the yield and the prices of crops in the various provinces. As regards the value of agricultural produce, two methods were available for that part of the total cropped area for which statistics neither of yield or prices can be obtained. The one usually adopted by investigators (e.g. Shah and Khambhata, D. L. Dubey, etc.) is to resort to a text book of agriculture such as Mollison's or Mukerjee's and obtain an

[1] For jowar, bajra, gram, barley and ragi, the figures given in the "Index Number of Indian Prices" are retail prices.

average yield per acre for minor food grains, etc., and separate figures of the value of fruits, vegetables, etc., are also worked out under this method. But the possibilities of error this method contains are many, and I have adopted the alternative method of applying to "the remaining area" the annual value per acre obtained from the figures of the value of agricultural produce of that part of the area under crops for which statistics are available. It is true that "the remaining area" contains the comparatively cheaper "other grains," and also the more valuable "fruits and vegetables," but the area under the latter is very small compared to that under the former and the value we apply may be a good average. But we may notice that this device to which we are compelled to resort makes for an understatement of the value of our agricultural produce.

Livestock.

A quinquennial census of cattle is undertaken in every province (in Burma and Central Provinces they have an annual census) and we get the number of cattle under different heads. The only other publication of the Government on livestock is the "Journal of Animal Husbandry," which contains technical articles on the matter of cattle improvement. No official figures are issued of milk yield, of slaughter for meat, of the production of hides and skins, bones, horns, manure, etc.

In the absence of official statistics of yield, we have

to obtain a figure which will give the average yield of milk. We have obtained such a figure on the basis of personal discussions with the Principal and Professor of Agriculture at the College in Poona, and on that of estimates made in a publication of the All India Cow Conference. An alternative figure is obtained on the basis of estimated consumption, and a final figure is then compiled to represent the value of milk yield.

Similar methods are employed for evaluating the production of meat, hides and skins, bones, horns, wool, etc., and statistics of export of these articles are also taken into account in arriving at the final figures of value. I should like to draw particular attention to my figures of the income arising from livestock, as it is the first comprehensive attempt to tackle this vexed question in the history of the attempts at estimating the Indian National Income.

Forests and Mineral Produce.

Statistics of quantity of the output of forest and mineral produce are available, and these can be supplemented by figures of exports. Figures of value are available for the major part of such output.

Industry.

We have already seen that there is no census of industrial production. The Government of India issues a biennial publication on " Large Scale Industrial Establishments in India," from which we obtain figures of the number of men employed by the organised or factory industries classified under different heads. We also get from official publications statistics of quantities of output of cotton and jute industries but not their values. Annual reports issued by the Bombay Mill Owners' Association, Indian Jute Mills' Association, and Indian Tea Association, all contain useful figures. The reports of the Tariff Board on various industries contain a miscellaneous amount of information of a useful kind. Figures of exports and imports are also relevant in determining industrial values.

No statistics are available of either output or values of cottage industries, which account for the larger portion of the population employed by industries. A survey of cottage industries has been made in the Madras Presidency by a special officer appointed for the purpose, but the reports do not contain statistics of output or value. There are miscellaneous reports issued by some of the Provincial Governments, e.g. a report on Handloom Weaving in the Bombay Presidency and one on Tanning in the Presidency, both issued by the Department of Industries. The main source of information and of a very indirect kind is the census report. A certain amount of information can be obtained from the different village studies which have been made in the past, as also from some of the evidence before the Royal Commission on Labour. But it must be admitted that such figures of the value of industrial production as we may arrive at will contain a considerable element of error.

Transport and Trade.

There are available figures of the revenues of railways classified under various sources. No statistics of income are available for vehicles of road transport, and a figure has to be estimated for the same from indirect evidence.

No figures again are available for trades, except statistics of the number employed in trade which we obtain from the census occupational tables. An estimate has again to be made on indirect evidence and due allowance has to be made both for the portion of produce which is not traded, and the turnover of the portion which is. It is not possible to arrive at a figure on the basis of the margin between harvest and wholesale prices because on examination there seems to be no rational relationship between the statistics of different price levels in this country. It must therefore be conceded that the valuation of income from trade and transport will be subject to a considerable margin of error.

Public Force and Administration.

Following Mr. Clark, we propose to include in the national dividend the income to the community represented by the essential functions of Government. The figures are obtained from the budget reports.

Professions and Liberal Arts.

No official statistics are available on the subject, nor, as we have already seen, income-tax statistics useful in this connection. Evidence of a very indirect character has to be used in evaluating this source of national income.

Domestic Servants.

Statistics of the number of domestic servants in the country are available and one can get an idea of the income contributed by them if we treat the annual value per head to be equal to that contributed by unskilled labourers.

We have seen what statistics are available in helping us to evaluate our national income, and it is obvious that methods have to be devised specially suited to our conditions, and the method we will employ can also generally be employed for estimating the national income of countries in the economic system of which agriculture predominates. We may therefore embark on a brief discussion of the method we shall use in estimating the national income.

Method.

We shall first endeavour to obtain an idea of the total number of incomes in the country classified under different occupational heads, for which our main source would be the census reports of 1921 and 1931. Having obtained a census of incomes, we shall endeavour to evaluate the industrial and agricultural output of the country; this figure will not merely be based on official statistics of output and prices, but in addition will be checked by consumption statistics. Incidentally, we may point out that figures gleaned from family budgets are highly useful for estimating income, particularly in countries of the size and economic character of India, and estimates based on these—provided the family budgets are representative—can even be compared for accuracy with those based on income-tax statistics and census of production. Against the value thus obtained we shall set off the number of incomes which can properly be held to be attributable to it. As for the remaining number and classes of incomes which cannot be accounted for by our census of production, we shall endeavour to obtain figures of 'average incomes' by applying which we shall be able to estimate the value of their contribution to the national dividend. The main source for getting these figures of 'average incomes' would be the wage censuses where available, family budgets and village surveys.

Finally, we shall try to estimate what portion of the total production is not available for human consumption, and this will include the part which goes for seeds, that which is fed to cattle, wastages, imports of raw materials, income due to foreigners, and that necessary for maintaining intact the capital equipment of the country. In making these calculations it will be more practicable and less conducive to error if we were to treat the source of income of the country as a whole and not try to find out the items and values to be debited against each source. Deducting the total amount thus arrived at from the total value of our gross output of utilities in the year, we shall obtain the figure of the net national dividend.

The Period.

We may conclude this chapter by pointing out that our calculations will be for the quinquennium 1925-29. Figures for any one year, however well chosen, are apt to lead to misleading conclusions, but if a post-war period has to be chosen, 1925-29 very nearly chooses itself. The years 1919 and early 1920 are years of boom followed by the slump the effects of which lasted almost up to 1925; after 1929 we get the great depression the end of which is not yet in evidence. The period 1925-29 is central and intermediate to the period 1919-34; it is free from the abnormal influences of slumps and booms, and on the whole those years can be taken to represent the "normal state" of our agricultural and manufacturing industries. Since 1929, of course, the situation has changed and manufacturing industries are comparatively better off than the agricultural industry, but if we desire to obtain a figure which can be taken as representative of our economic conditions, we cannot choose the slump period. And once a figure is obtained which can in some sense be treated as normal, it is not difficult to compile a series showing changes from year to year on the basis of an index of national prosperity calculated on the lines (with suitable modifications) followed by Sir William Beveridge in his "Unemployment." We shall therefore arrive at a figure of national income in our work which will be the annual average of the five years 1925-29.

Territory.

The figures dealt with in this work relate only to the British Provinces. Indian States have been left out of this study, because statistics available for the former are not all available for the latter.

Conclusion.

Finally, we may point out that this is a purely statistical and fact-finding investigation, and no attempt will be made either to institute international comparisons or to relate it to taxable capacity.

Chapter III

THE NUMBER OF INCOMES

The main source of our information is the census report, and we cannot call to our aid such supplementary figures as Mr. Clark can for England in the form of health and unemployment insurance statistics.

Table XVII of the " Imperial Tables " volume of the 1921 census report gives the figures of population according to occupation. The figures are classified under the five heads :—

Total Workers and Dependents.
Total Actual Workers—Males and Females.
Partially Agriculturist Workers—Males and Females.

Table X of the corresponding volume for 1931 gives the following classification :—

Total following Occupations—
  As Principal Occupation—Males and Females.
  As Working Dependents—Males and Females.
  As subsidiary to other occupations.

We can see that the classification has undergone considerable change in a decade. What we require is, first, a reduction of the 1921 and 1931 figures to a comparable form, and, second, an enumeration of the total number of incomes in the two periods.

The " total actual workers " of 1921 may be held to be comparable with the " total following occupations " of 1931, but this would not give the total number of incomes. The figure of 1921 includes persons who are following the occupations specified in the 1931 tables as subsidiary occupations; therefore, the number of persons following specified occupations as their principal occupations would be smaller, and there is a certain element of double counting. The census of 1921 gives statistics of persons belonging to other than the agricultural industry who are following agriculture as a subsidiary occupation; and this has to be deducted from the figure of the total of actual workers. But it gives no figures of persons whose principal occupation is agriculture, but who are also following subsidiary occupations of a non-agricultural kind. This figure has to be estimated and will have to be deducted before we can obtain the statistics of incomes or the number of principal workers in 1921.

For estimating this figure, we must have recourse to the statistics furnished in 1931 of persons who, in addition to a principal occupation, also have subsidiary occupations. Such persons numbered 1,10,88,000, of which 53,61,000 were following agriculture as a subsidiary occupation. The remaining workers who were following non-agricultural occupations as subsidiary callings numbered 57,27,000. Assuming that the increase in this number as from 1921 is of the same order of magnitude as in the case of the total population, we get 52,63,000 as the corresponding figure for 1921. This figure has to be deducted from the number of non-agricultural workers in 1921. We are now in a position to estimate the total number of incomes in 1921 and 1931.

TABLE 1

(In thousands)

	1921.	1931.
Total following occupations . . .	11,36,26	12,74,31
„ having subsidiary occupations .	74,63	1,10,88
„ persons following principal occupations	10,61,63	11,63,43

We can similarly classify the number of holders of incomes under the several census occupational heads. But we require figures for the years 1925-29, and we have to find the annual average figure for that period. The so-called natural rate of increase which is applied to movements during an intercensal period is the rate of increase during the previous period. But this can not be applied to this decade as the population has increased by more than 10 per cent. between 1921 and 1931, whereas the rate of increase during the previous decade was only 1·6 per cent. We shall, therefore, proceed on the assumption that the increase in the population is evened out between the ten years. This method is not quite so accurate, and it would be more correct to use the formula which assumes a uniform *rate* of increase, but actually there is not much difference between the figures obtained by these two methods, and it is simpler to use the former.

Working on this basis, we find the number of incomes in our period to be 11,22,91,000 or roughly

112·3 millions. This figure consists of the principal workers in the following occupations :—

TABLE 2

(In thousands)

1.	Exploitation of animals and vegetation	7,94,50
2.	" minerals	2,51
3.	" industry	1,08,98
4.	" transport	15,69
5.	" trade	54,52
6.	Public force and administration	10,91
7.	Professions and liberal arts	14,91
8.	Persons living on their income	1,25
9.	Domestic servants	57,63
10.	Persons whose occupations are insufficiently described	50,61
11.	Unproductive occupations	11,40
	Total	11,22,91

These figures exclude those who are following in addition to a principal occupation also some other subsidiary occupation or occupations. On the other hand, they include working dependents, who cannot naturally be expected to be making as much contribution to the national dividend per head as those adults who are whole-time principal employees. This omission of subsidiary workers and inclusion of working dependents does not matter for that part of the total number of incomes which will be accounted for by our census of production. But it becomes relevant when we are making up our figure of values by applying to the number of incomes an average per head ; this, however, is not likely to introduce any significant error, for the excess which may be due to over-estimation of the income of working dependents is balanced by the omission of the incomes of those who are following the occupations enumerated above as subsidiary callings. We may, therefore, reasonably assume that the total national income of the community during the period is to be found in the sum-total of the incomes of 112·3 millions, or, alternatively, in order to find the national income during the period, we are in quest of 112·3 million incomes.

There is, however, a qualification to our statement. Under the census head "Persons who were following occupations insufficiently described," we find the considerable figure of about 51 lakhs. A sub-head "Labourers and workmen otherwise unspecified" accounts for nearly 90 per cent. of the figure. We may also take into consideration the fact that the figures of the population supported by agriculture proper seem to have undergone a slight reduction which may possibly be accounted for by the rather considerable increase under this head. Accordingly, we may distribute 46 lakhs out of the 51 among the three census heads, exploitation of animals and vegetation, industry and domestic servants, on the basis of their relative importance as seen in the number of people following these occupations. The other 5 lakhs are obviously to be assigned to industry, as they consist of manufacturers, businessmen, contractors, cashiers, accountants, etc. We have, therefore, to add to the number of persons following each of these three occupations, 37·66, 10·22 and 2·73 lakhs respectively.

Then again, two of the census heads, viz. items 8 and 11, have to be ignored when we are considering incomes from a productive point of view. Both people who are living on their income and those who are following unproductive occupations (such as beggars, inmates of jails, asylums, etc.), are claimants on the national dividend, and have to be taken into account when considering problems of distribution. But they add nothing to the national income and have therefore no place in the number of incomes whose annual valuation we are in quest of.

We can now rearrange the number of incomes which make up the national dividend under the following heads :—[1]

TABLE 3

	(In thousands)
1. Exploitation of animals and vegetation .	8,32,16
2. ,, minerals . . .	2,51
3. ,, industry . . .	1,19,20
4. ,, transport . . .	15,69
5. ,, trade	54,52
6. Public force and administration . .	10,91
7. Professions and liberal arts . . .	14,91
8. Domestic servants	60,36
Total . .	11,10,26

[1] If we obtain statistics of the total population during the intercensal period by adding the excess of births over deaths every year, we get the following figures for our period :—

	(millions)
1924-25 . . .	253
1925-26 . . .	257
1926-27 . . .	259
1927-28 . . .	262
1928-29 . . .	264

giving an average of 260 millions. If we assume the working population to hold the same proportion as in 1931, we get 111·3 millions as the figure of actual workers—a figure which closely agrees with our figure of 111 millions.

Chapter IV

INCOME FROM EXPLOITATION OF ANIMALS AND VEGETATION—AGRICULTURE

We shall consider the income accruing from the exploitation of animals and vegetation under the following heads :—

Agriculture,
Livestock,
Fishing and Hunting.

In this chapter we shall endeavour to evaluate the agricultural output of the country. As we have already seen, statistics of area and yield are available by provinces for the majority of crops, and we shall proceed to consider the more important of these below.

Rice.

Rice is the most important of the Indian crops, covering as it does an average area of 80 million acres, which is very nearly a third of the total area under cultivation. It is generally regarded as a winter crop, being sown in the month of May to August and harvested in December and January. It forms the staple food of the people of the provinces of Madras, Bengal, Bihar and Orissa, Burma and parts of Bombay, and is used to some extent all over the country. We accordingly also find that it occupies a dominant place in the agricultural economy of Bengal (20 million acres), Bihar and Orissa (14 millions), Burma (13 millions), and Madras (11 millions). Punjab is the only province which shows no area under rice. The following two tables give statistics of yield and values, the latter being based, as previously mentioned by us, on harvest prices :—

TABLE 4

OUTPUT

(In thousands of tons)

Province.	1925-26.	1926-27.	1927-28.	1928-29.	1929-30.
Assam . .	15,88	15,36	13,08	16,77	13,46
Bengal . .	82,18	73,55	64,93	96,84	82,02
Bihar and Orissa .	48,89	47,88	43,78	55,88	60,11
Bombay . .	12,69	13,54	13,29	14,59	12,83
C.P. and Berar .	47,43	51,12	48,86	48,94	49,86
Madras . .	53,22	47,42	50,83	51,97	52,55
U.P. . . .	21,59	23,41	21,83	11,04	15,23
Burma . .	47,43	51,12	48,86	48,94	49,86

TABLE 5

VALUE

(In thousands of Rs.)

Province.	1925-26.	1926-27.	1927-28.	1928-29.	1929-30.
Bengal .	156,96,38	144,15,80	132,45,72	175,28,04	134,51,28
Bihar and Orissa .	75,29,06	81,39,60	73,11,26	94,99,60	81,74,96
Madras .	103,24,68	94,36,58	100,64,34	97,18,39	89,76,66
Burma .	38,78,98	49,98,56	40,06,52	37,68,38	31,41,18
U.P. . .	42,74,82	46,35,18	42,35,02	22,19,04	29,08,93
Bombay .	28,29,87	30,46,50	28,98,22	31,71,22	26,81,57
C.P. . .	21,93,26	28,57,52	24,99,20	25,50,84	27,16,24
Assam .	1,35,00	1,00,80	92,38	96,43	67,30
Total . (in lakhs of Rs.)	468,62	475,40	443,53	485,52	421,18

The annual average value of rice during the period thus comes to about Rs. 459 crores. This does not include the value of the rice produced in the minor provinces and other administered areas (e.g. Ajmer-Merwara, Coorg, Baluchistan, etc.). Actually, however, rice is grown only in Coorg, and the value of its production is hardly more than Rs. 3 lakhs.

Wheat.

Wheat is the next most important single crop, as it occupies an area of a little more than 24 million acres. It is generally a *rabi* crop, sown from October to December and harvested from March to May. It forms the staple food of the populations of the Punjab, the United Provinces, and parts of Central Provinces and Bombay. It occupies a dominant place in the Punjab (9·6 million acres), The United Provinces (7 millions) and the Central Provinces (3·4 millions). There is no area under wheat in the Provinces of Burma, Madras and Assam. The following two tables give statistics of yield and value :—

TABLE 6

OUTPUT

(In thousands of tons)

Province.	1925-26.	1926-27.	1927-28.	1928-29.	1929-30.
Bengal . .	28	32	22	32	33
Bihar and Orissa .	4,27	4,77	4,18	5,13	4,54
Bombay . .	2,85	3,18	3,95	4,06	4,30
C.P. and Berar .	8,81	7,73	5,91	5,18	5,88
N.W.F. . .	2,68	2,94	1,61	2,31	2,48
Punjab . .	29,36	29,46	23,44	30,70	37,81
U.P. . .	22,87	24,92	23,61	24,80	33,09

TABLE 7

VALUE

(In thousands of Rs.)

Province.	1925-26.	1926-27	1927-28.	1928-29.	1929-30.
Bombay .	5,95,65	6,77,34	6,47,80	7,95,76	6,88,00
U.P. . .	28,13,01	34,38,96	32,54,57	35,21,60	35,07,54
Bihar and Orissa .	7,42,98	8,20,44	6,85,52	8,41,32	7,00,40
Bengal .	55,80	54,40	37,74	52,48	52,80
Punjab .	44,88,20	42,02,98	31,96,68	39,60,22	34,36,53
C.P. . .	11,71,73	11,90,42	8,33,31	7,62,20	7,11,48
N.W.F. .	3,35,72	3,55,74	1,86,76	2,02,61	2,45,52
Total . (in lakhs of Rs.)	102,04	107,40	88,42	101,36	93,42

The value of wheat produced in Delhi and Ajmer-Merwara is practically negligible, hardly amounting to Rs. 2 lakhs. The annual average value of wheat produced during this period thus comes to very nearly Rs. 100 crores.

Jowar.

Jowar is both a *rabi* and a *kharif* crop and has an exclusively domestic market. It forms the staple food of the mass of the population of the Bombay Presidency, and is also used extensively in Madras, Central Provinces and United Provinces. Thus we find the crop occupying large areas in Bombay (8·3 millions acres), Madras (4·7 millions), Central Provinces (4·6 millions), and United Provinces (2·3 millions). The following tables give figures of yield and value :—

TABLE 8

OUTPUT

(In thousands of tons)

Province.	1925-26.	1926-27.	1927-28.	1928-29.	1929-30.
Bengal . .	1	1	1	1	1
Bihar and Orissa .	22	17	18	21	26
Bombay . .	15,66	14,73	18,31	17,56	17,52
Burma . .	44	79	68	60	50
C.P. and Berar .	7,63	8,88	9,94	11,09	10,36
Punjab . .	1,00	1,07	1,26	90	75
U.P. . .	4,00	4,00	5,24	5,57	3,34
Madras . .	12,92	12,11	13,39	13,63	14,83

The North-West Frontier Province, Ajmer-Merwara and Delhi produce on an average a total of about 20 thousand tons every year.

TABLE 9

VALUE

(In thousands of Rs.)

Province.	1925-26.	1926-27.	1927-28.	1928-29.	1929-30.
Bombay .	20,82,78	20,03,28	22,70,44	21,24,76	22,60,08
U.P. . .	5,32,00	5,44,96	4,56,74	4,74,28	6,81,58
Madras .	15,89,16	14,89,53	16,60,36	15,53,82	14,68,17
Bihar and Orissa .	58,30	44,71	40,86	55,23	48,36
Burma .	1,16,60	2,07,77	1,54,36	1,37,80	93,00
Punjab .	1,17,40	1,05,59	1,09,33	1,05,63	98,00
C.P. and Berar .	8,16,41	10,12,32	11,53,04	12,86,44	9,63,48
Total .	53,12,65	54,08,36	58,45,13	57,37,46	56,12,67

The annual average value of the jowar produced during this period thus comes to about Rs. 56 crores.

Bajra.

Bajra and jowar form the staple diet of the Indian poor, and like jowar, bajra is also a purely domestic crop. Again, bajra is dominant in the Bombay Presidency (5·1 million acres), and is found extensively in Madras (3·3 millions) and United Provinces (1·9 millions). It is not so much in evidence in Central Provinces (0·1 million), while it takes the place of jowar in the Punjab (2·7 millions). The following tables give figures of yield and value :—

TABLE 10

OUTPUT

(In thousands of tons)

Province.	1925-26.	1926-27.	1927-28.	1928-29.	1929-30.
Bihar and Orissa .	25	25	30	27	27
Bombay . .	5,43	7,91	7,60	7,07	5,04
C.P. and Berar .	23	24	27	33	26
Madras . .	8,19	7,83	8,36	8,29	7,61
Punjab . .	2,78	3,63	3,33	2,47	2,82
U.P. . . .	2,71	4,45	4,01	2,66	3,66

The North-West Frontier Province and Delhi together produce about 22 thousand tons every year.

TABLE 11

VALUE

(In thousands of Rs.)

Province.	1925-26.	1926-27.	1927-28.	1928-29.	1929-30.
Bombay .	6,57,03	9,41,29	9,72,80	9,68,59	6,35,04
U.P. .	3,84,82	4,85,05	3,96,99	4,49,54	4,42,86
Madras .	10,48,32	10,41,39	11,28,60	10,69,41	8,82,76
Bihar and Orissa .	77,50	68,50	82,20	84,24	56,97
Punjab .	3,31,12	3,76,74	3,51,27	3,40,40	3,07,07
C.P. . .	71,30	65,76	73,98	1,02,96	54,86
N.W.F. .	24,84	16,35	14,28	16,56	28,86
Total .	25,96,93	29,95,08	30,20,12	30,31,74	27,08,42

The average annual value of the bajra produced during the period comes therefore to about Rs. 29 crores.

Gram.

Gram is a *rabi* crop and covers an area of a little more than 13·5 million acres. It is a very important

TABLE 12

OUTPUT

(In thousands of tons)

Province.	1925-26.	1926-27.	1927-28.	1928-29.	1929-30.
Bengal . .	32	34	18	42	46
Bihar and Orissa .	5,29	5,61	4,30	4,42	5,33
Bombay . .	97	1,07	1,36	1,15	1,19
Burma . .	24	40	48	33	32
C.P. . . .	2,85	2,25	1,78	1,53	2,19
Madras . .	26	8	15	16	16
Punjab . .	7,60	11,99	8,58	7,26	7,63
U.P. . . .	20,70	17,72	15,01	10,65	12,47

crop in the United Provinces (5·6 million acres), and is also found to a considerable extent in the Punjab (3·9 millions), Bihar and Orissa (1·4 millions) and Central Provinces and Berar (1·2 millions). Tables 12 and 13 give figures of output and value.

The North-West Frontier Province and Delhi are responsible for an output of 34 thousand tons.

TABLE 13

VALUE

(In thousands of Rs.)

Province.	1925-26.	1926-27.	1927-28.	1928-29.	1929-30.
Bombay .	1,53,26	1,73,34	1,87,68	2,08,15	2,05,87
U.P. . .	21,52,80	19,66,92	17,41,16	15,44,25	13,21,82
Madras .	66,82	21,12	41,70	51,20	34,88
Bihar and Orissa .	6,40,09	7,62,96	5,80,50	6,63,00	7,24,88
Burma .	26,64	42,40	39,36	37,62	31,68
Bengal .	42,56	42,64	28,26	63,00	62,56
Punjab .	8,40,21	12,23,48	10,39,49	9,26,41	7,52,93
C.P. . .	3,02,10	2,85,75	2,10,04	2,12,67	2,49,56
N.W.F. .	38,80	26,22	27,00	23,12	31,61
Total .	42,63,28	45,45,33	38,95,19	35,29,42	34,15,89

The annual average value of the gram produced during the period comes to a little more than Rs. 39 crores.

Barley and Maize.

During the period the average area under barley and maize was 6·8 and 5·9 million acres respectively. Barley is not found all over the country, but is practically confined to the United Provinces (4·2 million acres), Punjab (0·9 million acres) and Bihar and Orissa (1·3 million acres). It is also an inportant crop in the North-West Frontier Province. Maize is a little more extensively distributed, but the important centres again are the United Provinces (1·9 million acres), Bihar and Orissa (1·6 million acres), and the Punjab (1 million acres), and, like barley, it is a very important crop in the North-West Frontier Province. The following tables give figures of output and value :—

TABLE 14

(In thousands)

	Barley.		Maize.	
	Output (tons).	Value (Rs.).	Output (tons).	Value (Rs.).
1925-26 . .	25,62	26,13,88	18,68	20,81,10
1926-27 . .	25,33	26,20,07	19,03	19,43,70
1927-28 . .	20,70	19,72,44	19,69	20,91,70
1928-29 . .	24,86	26,72,02	16,85	23,76,86
1929-30 . .	22,76	18,52,04	21,47	24,06,63

The annual average value of barley and maize produced during the period thus amounts to about Rs. 24 and 22 crores respectively.

Sugar Cane.

The importance of the sugar cane crop has been drawn attention to by the Tariff Board on sugar who make the importance of the agricultural side of it one of the grounds for their recommending protection to sugar. The area under this crop during our period was on the average 26,42,000 acres, the United Provinces claiming a lion's share (14,62 thousand acres), the Punjab (409 thousand acres) and Bihar and Orissa (288 thousand acres) coming next. This crop is largely an irrigated crop, as can be seen from the fact that in 1929-30, 16,91 thousand acres, or nearly 70 per cent. of the area under sugar cane, was under irrigation. The following tables give figures of output of raw sugar and its value :—

TABLE 15

YIELD

(In thousands of tons)

Province.	1925-26.	1926-27.	1927-28.	1928-29.	1929-30.
Assam	35	42	42	40	26
Bengal	2,45	2,15	2,36	2,16	2,20
Bihar and Orissa	3,18	3,03	3,09	3,13	3,04
Bombay	1,85	1,84	2,03	1,86	1,75
C.P. and Berar	29	28	36	37	36
Madras	3,15	3,05	2,83	2,45	2,75
N.W.F.	59	62	63	59	63
Punjab	3,03	3,49	3,81	2,89	2,04
U.P.	14,12	16,80	15,22	12,10	13,01

The annual average value of the sugar produced during this period amounts to a little more than Rs. 57 crores.

Without counting the value of the minor food grains and that of special food crops like fruits and vegetables, the total annual value of the food crops grown in this country comes on an average to Rs. 786 crores.

TABLE 16

VALUE

(In thousands of Rs.)

Province.	1925-26.	1926-27.	1927-28.	1928-29.	1929-30.
Bombay .	5,55,00	4,54,48	4,62,84	5,04,06	4,44,50
Assam .	83,65	94,50	86,52	83,20	55,38
Bengal .	6,68,85	5,37,35	5,71,12	5,03,28	4,75,20
Bihar and Orissa .	6,70,98	5,42,37	6,63,00	5,47,55	5,38,08
C.P. and Berar .	61,24	50,07	61,31	64,90	63,66
Madras .	8,11,44	8,77,00	6,14,90	7,13,44	7,39,20
N.W.F. .	1,22,72	1,18,42	1,15,92	1,09,74	1,17,18
Punjab .	5,92,80	5,40,34	5,63,96	4,72,03	3,36,67
U.P. . .	29,81,97	30,04,30	25,92,16	21,22,61	23,00,53
Total .	65,48,65	62,18,83	57,31,73	51,20,81	50,70,40

Cotton.

Cotton is probably the most important commercial crop grown in India. It is found in all the provinces. There are two crops, early cotton being grown mainly in Central and Northern India and late cotton in Southern and Western India, and the sowing season thus extends altogether from March to August and the harvesting season from October to April.

The area under cotton during our period amounted on an average to 16·3 million acres, of which Bombay and the Central Provinces and Berar claimed 5 millions each, the Punjab 2·4 millions and Madras 2 millions. The amount of cotton exported during the period was on an average 35,91 thousand bales (400 lbs.), while the total amount produced in British India was only 35,64 thousand bales, and there is a large domestic consumption. This apparently curious fact is explained when we remember that the Indian States account for a good deal of the total cotton produced in India. As a matter of fact, British India accounts for only 63 per cent. of the total output of Indian cotton, while 64 per cent. of the total crop is exported.

Then again, we find, on examination, a great disparity in the value of cotton produced and cotton harvested. This is partly due to the fact that exports are partly accounted for by Indian States, while it is also due to the higher value per bale of cotton exported as compared with the harvest value per bale of cotton produced. These two figures work out at Rs. 185 and Rs. 150 per bale respectively. This difference is a result partly of the exported cotton being of a better quality, and partly of marketing charges which have to be incurred before the cotton is shipped for export.

Moreover, the figure of output of cotton that we obtain from the " area and the yield " statistics are an underestimate of the actual crop. The Indian Central Cotton Committee compiles figures of export and mill consumption and of extra factory consumption, and, comparing these figures with those given in the agricultural statistics, we find, that the former exceed the latter by a little more than 13 per cent., and we have, therefore, added 13 per cent. to the total figures of value of cotton produced in British India.

The following tables give statistics of yield and value.

TABLE 17

(In bales of 400 lbs., Figures in thousands)

Province.	1925-26.	1926-27.	1927-28.	1928-29.	1929-30.
Assam . . .	13	15	15	17	15
Bengal . . .	23	23	17	15	18
Bihar and Orissa . .	15	14	14	14	13
Bombay . . .	10,46	7,48	9,79	10,49	7,89
Burma . . .	83	73	67	56	67
C.P. and Berar . .	9,80	9,77	12,35	13,34	12,52
Madras . . .	5,65	3,86	4,44	5,24	5,09
Punjab . . .	7,90	5,18	5,14	5,24	7,00
U.P.	2,75	2,57	1,96	2,52	2,86
Rest of British India .	25	21	17	26	16
Add 13 per cent. to cover deficit in estimates . . .	4,96	3,94	4,55	4,95	4,76
Total yield .	43,11	34,26	39,53	43,06	41,41

TABLE 18

VALUE

(In thousands of Rs.)

Province.	1925-26.	1926-27.	1927-28.	1928-29.	1929-30.
Bombay . .	17,49,82	11,19,56	15,76,19	15,73,50	9,86,25
U.P. . . .	4,86,75	3,88,07	3,97,88	4,30,92	3,63,22
Madras . .	10,07,13	5,85,88	9,07,41	5,45,88	6,51,51
Bihar and Orissa .	29,50	21,56	21,56	21,84	17,62
Assam . .	23,01	22,65	30,45	29,07	19,05
Burma . .	1,46,91	1,10,23	1,36,01	95,76	85,09
Bengal . .	53,04	48,00	38,20	28,44	32,34
Punjab . .	13,98,30	7,82,18	10,43,42	8,96,04	8,89,00
C.P. and Berar .	15,19,00	12,21,25	19,01,90	18,27,58	12,64,52
N.W.F. . .	12,39	7,55	4,06	6,84	5,08
Add 13 per cent. to cover deficit in estimates . .	8,32,88	6,59,90	7,87,42	7,09,26	5,60,78
Total .	72,39,63	49,66,83	68,44,50	61,65,13	48,74,46

The average value of the cotton produced during our period thus comes to a little more than Rs. 60 crores.

Jute.

Jute is, as is well known, a very important money crop of the Bengali cultivator, and we have the world's monopoly of producing it. It is an autumn crop, being sown from March to May and harvested in August and September. The area under this crop during our period came on an average to 3·36 million acres, which was distributed among Bengal (2·93 million acres), Bihar and Orissa (·25 million acres), and Assam (·16 million acres). As for cotton, similarly for jute, certain estimates (given in the report of the Indian Jute Mills' Association) are available of exports, mill consumption and extra factory consumption, and the figure thus obtained is, on an average, 3 per cent. more than the figures obtained from the "Area and Yield" reports, and 3 per cent. has therefore to be added both to the yield and value figures. The following tables give figures of yield and value :—

TABLE 19

YIELD

(In bales of 400 lbs.—figures in thousands)

Province.	1925.	1926.	1927.	1928.	1929.
Assam . .	2,79	5,99	4,66	6,24	3,52
Bengal . .	79,42	1,06,38	89,96	85,14	91,87
Bihar and Orissa .	6,40	7,64	6,67	6,93	7,19
Add 3 per cent. to cover deficit in estimates . .	2,66	3,60	3,04	2,95	3,08
Total yield .	91,27	1,23,61	1,04,33	1,01,26	1,05,66

TABLE 20

VALUE

(In thousands of Rs.)

Province.	1925.	1926.	1927.	1928.	1929.
Assam . .	3,31,89	4,13,31	3,44,84	4,18,08	1,86,56
Bengal . .	71,55,90	42,60,80	36,01,60	36,63,17	34,92,20
Bihar and Orissa .	5,69,60	2,44,48	2,20,11	2,63,34	2,73,52
Add 3 per cent. to cover deficit in estimates . .	2,41,72	1,47,56	1,25,00	1,30,34	1,18,57
Total .	82,99,11	50,66,15	42,91,55	44,74,93	40,70,85

Jute is an important export crop, nearly 41 per cent. of the total crop having been exported in a raw state during the period under discussion. The average value of the exports of raw jute came to Rs. 31 crores, and the disparity of values between the export figures and those of harvest values is due to the fact that while the harvest value per bale of jute was Rs. 50 during our period, that per bale of exported jute was Rs. 71. This difference is one result of causes similar to those we have already discussed with regard to a similar phenomenon in the case of cotton.

The annual average value of the output of jute amounted during this period to Rs. 52,40,52 thousands or a little more than Rs. 52 crores. The total annual average value of fibres, excepting for minor fibres, thus came to more than Rs. 112 crores.

Oil-seeds : Groundnut.

The groundnut crop has been growing in importance during the last few years, the area cultivated with it having very nearly doubled itself during the last ten years, and its importance as an export crop has also been increasing during the same period. In fact, it is the latter fact which has led to its growing popularity as a money crop, particularly in Bombay and Madras, and to the rapid increase in its area. It is usually sown from May to August and harvested from November to February. The total area under this crop during this period averaged to 4·45 million acres, of which Madras claimed 3·10 million acres, Bombay ·80 million acres, and Burma ·55 million acres. The following tables give figures of yield and value :—

TABLE 21

YIELD
(In thousands of tons.)

Province.	1925-26.	1926-27.	1927-28.	1928-29.	1929-30.
Bombay . .	2,75	3,13	3,98	5,26	4,26
Burma . .	1,65	1,65	1,45	1,60	1,90
Madras . .	12,64	12,07	16,71	18,30	15,22

TABLE 22

VALUE
(In thousands of Rs.)

Province.	1925-26.	1926-27.	1927-28.	1928-29.	1929-30.
Bombay .	7,28,75	8,13,80	9,75,10	12,93,96	9,75,54
Burma .	2,02,95	2,78,85	2,27,15	1,93,60	2,88,80
Madras .	33,69,60	31,38,20	40,93,95	45,01,80	34,85,38
Total .	43,01,30	42,30,85	52,96,20	59,89,36	47,49,72

The annual average value of exports (including those from the Indian States) during the period was Rs. 14·6 crores (the quantity was 588 thousand tons), while the average value of production in British India was a little more than Rs. 49 crores.

Rape and Mustard.

Rape and mustard are generally sown together, and very often—particularly in the United Provinces—

TABLE 23

YIELD

(In thousands of tons)

Province.	1925-26.	1926-27.	1927-28.	1928-29.	1929-30.
Assam	74	72	69	66	62
Bengal	84	1,32	1,16	1,23	1,34
Bihar and Orissa	1,62	1,60	1,53	1,78	1,62
Bombay	14	19	16	12	40
N.W.F.	11	9	9	10	9
Punjab	1,25	1,47	1,50	1,62	1,50
U.P.	4,28	4,49	2,96	3,50	5,23

they constitute a favourite mixed crop. As a matter of fact, this fact makes the figures of area and yield for the United Provinces highly conjectural. They are *rabi* crops and as such sown from August to October and harvested from January to April. The reported area under this crop during our period averaged to 5·87 million acres in the United Provinces, 1·08 million acres in the Punjab, and ·73 and ·72 million acres in Bengal and Bihar and Orissa respectively. In addition, there were 250 thousand acres sown with rape and mustard in Madras, Burma and Ajmer-Merwara, for which no statistics of yield are available. Very little mustard is exported, but a fair amount of rape seed (75 thousand tons) is exported to the value of Rs. 128 lakhs. Tables 23 and 24 give figures of yield and value.

TABLE 24

VALUE

(In thousands of Rs.)

Province.	1925-26.	1926-27.	1927-28.	1928-29.	1929-30.
Bombay .	34,16	43,89	36,96	28,68	87,60
Bihar and Orissa .	3,53,16	3,48,80	3,33,54	3,79,14	3,22,38
Assam .	1,50,96	1,39,68	1,33,86	1,23,42	1,15,94
Bengal .	2,17,56	3,24,72	2,85,36	2,93,92	3,04,18
U.P. . .	10,44,32	10,37,19	6,83,76	8,36,50	11,45,37
Punjab .	2,72,22	3,15,06	2,98,59	3,03,19	2,42,03
N.W.F. .	18,15	14,76	11,52	16,40	11,16
Total .	20,90,53	22,24,10	17,83,59	19,81,30	22,28,66

The annual average value of the rape and mustard produced during this period came to Rs. 20,61,64 thousands or to a little less than Rs. 21 crores.

Linseed, Sesamum and Castor.

I am taking all these three seeds together not because they have some natural connection but because none of them yields an output valued at more than Rs. 10 crores. Linseed is a *rabi* crop being sown from August to October and harvested from January to April; sesamum is a *kharif* crop being sown from May to July and harvested from October to December; castor seed, though sown from May to July, is only harvested in January and February. The total area under linseed was on an average 28,08 thousand acres, of which 9,50 thousands were in the Central Provinces and Berar, 9,38 thousands were in the United Provinces (including a large mixed area), and 6,49 thousands in Bihar and Orissa. Sesamum had an area of 41,98 thousand acres, but was found in almost all the provinces, Burma leading with an acreage of 11,21 thousand acres. As regards castor seed, the area was 5,32 thousand acres, of which a lion's share of 3,45 thousand went to the province of Madras. Of these, sesamum was not much of an export crop. Linseed, however, is an important export crop, the average figures for our period being 225 thousand tons and Rs. 513 lakhs; the average value of the exports of castor seed was Rs. 238 lakhs which was considerably in excess of the total value of the crop produced in British India; this however, is only an index of the importance of the crop in the Indian States, the area under castor seed in the Indian States in fact exceeding that in British India by 62 per cent. On the whole, we can regard castor seed and linseed as mainly money crops. The following tables give figures of yield and value of these three crops:—

TABLE 25

OUTPUT

(In thousands of tons)

	1925-26.	1926-27.	1927-28.	1928-29.	1929-30.
Linseed . . .	3,74	3,84	3,21	3,04	3,54
Sesamum . . .	3,50	3,38	4,07	3,90	3,79
Castor seed . .	71	57	71	59	53

TABLE 26

VALUE

(In thousands of Rs.)

	1925-26.	1926-27.	1927-28.	1928-29.	1929-30.
Linseed . .	7,82,05	7,76,36	6,15,17	5,78,63	7,49,94
Sesamum . .	9,27,33	8,80,90	9,07,97	8,95,04	8,27,46
Castor seed .	1,72,24	1,11,62	1,74,48	1,36,28	1,34,06

The annual average value of the yield of linseed seasmum and castor seed during the period thus amounted to 7 crores, 8·9 crores, and 1·4 crores respectively.

Without taking into account minor oil-seeds for which figures of yield and prices are not available, the total annual value of oil-seeds during this period came to Rs. 87 crores.

Tea and Coffee.

Tea is an important money crop, and it is distinguished in the agricultural economy, as tea plantations are mostly owned by foreigners and cultivators of a similar type for other crops are very few. The crop is usually plucked from May to December in Northern

India, while in the south it is plucked during the whole of the year. The total area under tea during our period was 6,91 thousand acres. Assam, of course, accounted for much the larger portion of this area (4,24 thousands), Bengal came a respectable second (1,91 thousands) and Madras had 58 thousand acres under tea. It is curious to note, that a certain amount of tea is grown in Burma, but it is used for consumption as pickles! Tea is mostly produced for purposes of export, nearly 97 per cent. of the total production being sent abroad, and during this period exports came to Rs. 28·3 crores every year. When comparing this figure with that of the value of domestic production, we must remember that part of the exports are from the production of Indian States (Travancore had 58 thousand acres under tea during this period), and that the value of the exported tea is a little higher than the internal price. It may finally be observed that no harvest prices of tea were available and we have used an average of the three types of tea for which wholesale prices are given in the "Index Number of Indian Prices." The following table gives figures of yield and value of tea during this period :—

TABLE 27

(In thousands)

	Output.	Value.
1925	334,871	29,30,12
1926	363,582	31,15,06
1927	361,154	26,71,04
1928	372,788	28,15,32
1929	400,758	26,50,85

The annual average value of the tea produced during the period thus came to Rs. 28,36,48 thousands, or a little more than Rs. 28 crores.

Coffee is grown mainly in Madras and Coorg among the British Provinces. The total area under coffee during the period was 73,000 acres, and the yield was 16·2 million lbs. valued at 1,23,04 thousand rupees on the basis of export values. The value of the tea and coffee produced every year thus comes to very nearly Rs. 30 crores.

Tobacco.

Tobacco is a crop which has been growing steadily in importance, and will undoubtedly continue to do so in the future as well. It is practically grown all over India, but more than 40 per cent. of the total area is found in Bengal and Madras. Statistics are not available for all the provinces for the first three years of our period, and have had to be worked out on the basis of the yield per acre obtained from the known figures of output. Harvest prices again are not available for most of the provinces, and there is such a disparity between the value per maund on the basis of harvest prices for Bihar and Orissa, and the value on the basis of export values, that we have been driven to accept a uniform compromise figure of Rs. 20 per bazaar maund as the value of tobacco during this period. The following table gives statistics of area, yield and output for tobacco during this period :—

TABLE 28

(In thousands)

	Area (acres).	Yield (tons).	Value (Rs.).
1925-26 . . .	10,64	4,67	25,29,82
1926-27 . . .	10,49	4,54	24,78,84
1927-28 . . .	11,40	5,88	32,10,48
1928-29 . . .	11,43	5,80	31,66,80
1929-30 . . .	11,67	6,07	33,13,82

The annual average value of tobacco comes to Rs. 29,39,95 thousands or nearly Rs. 30 crores.

Rubber.

Rubber is grown mainly in Madras and Burma. During our period the total area under rubber averaged to 96,000 acres and the yield to 13·2 million lbs. of dry rubber valued at Rs. 137 lakhs.

Indigo.

Indigo, once a very important crop, is still grown in India, and its main centres are Madras and the Punjab. The total area under indigo came to 89,000 acres during the period, and the yield was 17,000 cwts. of dye with a value of Rs. 83 lakhs.

Other Crops.

There still remain a great number of crops for which neither statistics of yield nor of price are available, and for many of them even detailed figures of area are not available, as most of them consist of the "remaining" or "other" items in a big sub-head. The following table gives relevant details, such as are available :—

TABLE 29

(In thousands of acres)

	1925-26.	1926-27.	1927-28.	1928-29.	1929-30.
Ragi	38,77	38,51	38,47	39,10	39,98
Other food grains .	2,86,69	2,90,81	2,95,20	2,95,81	2,92,25
Cocoanut . . .	10,36	9,56	9,98	10,46	9,65
Other seeds . .	8,25	9,17	9,35	9,73	9,77
Condiments and spices .	14,38	13,95	14,41	14,46	12,87
Other sugars . .	1,67	1,60	1,54	1,58	1,58
Other fibres . .	9,07	8,01	6,41	6,55	6,64
Other dyeing matter .	5,65	4,80	4,76	5,40	6,21
Cinchona . . .	3	3	3	2	2
Other drugs . .	1,46	1,38	1,51	1,41	1,39
Fodder crops . .	89,03	89,20	91,13	91,59	93,53
Fruits and vegetables .	51,61	49,26	50,69	40,92	51,81
Miscellaneous non-food crops . . .	10,67	10,57	10,80	10,35	10,83
Miscellaneous food crops	12,09	11,86	12,79	13,49	14,59
Total area for which statistics of neither yield nor price are available . . .	5,39,72	5,39,98	5,48,08	5,49,80	5,59,50

We have already pointed out that we are going to adopt an indirect method of valuing the annual output of this area, viz. applying to this area a value per acre based on statistics available for the remaining area under crops, and this method is employed separately for each province, as there is considerable variation in the value per acre between the different provinces. We are excluding from our valuation the output of the area under fodder crops, as otherwise we will have to deduct it when considering the value of the income from livestock, and our total figures of valuation of agricultural output will therefore be for agricultural output excluding fodder crops.

The following table contains figures of the area for which statistics of yield and price are not available, and the estimated valuation of the output of this area :—

TABLE 30

(Area in thousands of acres—Value in lakhs of Rs.)

	1925-26.		1926-27.		1927-28.		1928-29.		1929-30.	
	Area.	Value.	Area.	Value.	Area.	Value.	Area.	Value.	Area.	Value.
Assam .	8,18	3,78	8,25	3,51	8,21	3,69	8,94	3,35	8,67	2,17
Bengal .	23,40	16,54	23,28	19,67	22,56	17,67	23,63	21,51	24,11	28,66
Bihar and Orissa .	81,87	44,25	80,97	46,07	82,12	44,28	77,34	48,66	80,71	44,96
Bombay .	47,35	19,75	52,00	21,32	53,93	23,30	53,05	24,19	49,73	18,70
Burma .	20,07	5,93	20,97	7,69	23,54	6,89	21,65	5,94	22,50	5,33
C.P. and Berar .	54,60	16,70	56,31	18,97	56,83	19,04	57,75	21,83	59,28	18,08
Madras .	1,19,56	90,03	1,16,31	82,93	1,16,58	89,56	1,16,89	76,83	1,19,45	80,02
Punjab .	19,57	7,24	17,93	5,96	18,71	5,92	17,76	5,34	20,28	5,54
N.W.F. .	1,67	60	1,40	49	1,52	39	1,41	40	1,74	48
U.P. .	74,42	38,70	72,36	42,35	73,91	35,18	80,80	34,57	80,50	38,72
Total .	4,50,69	2,43,52	4,49,78	24,89,6	4,61,91	2,45,92	4,59,22	2,42,62	4,66,97	2,42,66

We are now in a position to evaluate the agricultural output of British India (excluding areas like Delhi,

Ajmer-Merwara and Coorg) during the period 1925-26 to 1929-30.[1] This is made up as under :—

TABLE 31

VALUE

(In lakhs of Rs.)

	1925-26.	1926-27.	1927-28.	1928-29.	1929-30.	Average for period.
Rice	4,68,62	4,75,40	4,43,53	4,85,52	4,21,18	4,58,85
Wheat	1,02,04	1,07,40	88,42	1,01,36	93,42	98,53
Jowar	53,13	54,08	58,45	57,37	56,13	55,83
Bajra	25,97	29,96	30,20	30,32	27,08	28,71
Barley	26,14	26,20	19,72	27,72	18,52	23,66
Maize	20,81	19,44	20,92	23,77	24,07	21,80
Gram	42,63	45,45	38,95	35,29	34,16	39,30
Sugar Cane	65,49	62,19	57,32	51,21	50,70	57,38
Cotton	72,40	49,77	68,45	61,65	48,74	60,20
Jute	82,99	50,66	42,92	44,75	40,71	52,41
Groundnut	43,01	42,31	52,96	59,89	47,50	49,13
Rape and mustard	20,91	22,24	17,84	19,81	22,29	20,62
Linseed	7,82	7,76	6,15	5,79	7,50	7,00
Seasamum	9,27	8,81	9,08	8,95	8,27	8,88
Castor seed	1,72	1,12	1,74	1,36	1,34	1,46
Tea	29,30	31,15	26,71	28,15	26,51	28,36
Coffee	1,23	1,23	1,23	1,23	1,23	1,23
Tobacco	25,30	24,79	32,10	31,67	33,14	29,40
Rubber	1,37	1,37	1,37	1,37	1,37	1,37
Indigo	83	83	83	83	83	83
Other crops	2,43,52	2,48,96	2,45,92	2,42,62	2,42,66	2,44,74
Total	13,44,50	13,11,12	12,64,81	13,20,63	12,07,35	12,89,68

The annual value of our agricultural production thus works out at Rs. 1290 crores. In the next chapter we

[1] This period does not strictly apply to all the crops included in the table. Crops like tea, jute, and one or two others have statistics furnished for them for only calendar years.

shall proceed to consider the value of our income from livestock, such as milk, milk products, meat, bones, hides and skins, etc., and then we shall be in a position to know the annual value of 83 million incomes which have "Exploitation of Animals and Vegetation" as their means of livelihood.[1]

[1] An independent check on our figures is obtained from the reports of the different provincial Banking Enquiry Reports, some of which contain estimates of the value of agricultural produce of their provinces. These figures are as under :—

	(In lakhs of Rs.)
Bengal	2,43,81
Madras	1,99,44
Bombay	1,53,00
Bihar and Orissa	1,12,00
Punjab	99,00
C.P. and Berar	79,17
	8,86,42

If we assume that the value of the agricultural produce of other provinces is on the same basis per head of population (the known figures cover 72·1 per cent. of the total population of British India in 1921 and 72·7 per cent. of that in 1931), we get Rs. 1224 crores as the value of the agricultural produce of British India, and this figure compares well with our figure of Rs. 1285 crores.

Chapter V

EXPLOITATION OF ANIMALS AND VEGETATION—LIVESTOCK

The contribution which livestock make to the national income takes the following forms :—

Labour in cultivation.
Milk and milk products.
Meat.
Hides and skins.
Wool.
Bones, horns, tips, etc.
Addition to livestock.
Manure.

It is very difficult to estimate properly the income from livestock, as statistics of yield are conspicuous by their almost complete absence. The only statistics available are of the number, by classes, of livestock in India computed from a quinquennial census of cattle which are taken in every British province. (Two provinces hold an annual census). A certain amount of indirect evidence is obtained by the figures of exports. It must be admitted that in the past sufficient importance has not been attached to the contribution which this factor makes ; and it has even been argued that the contribution which they make is balanced by the cost of their upkeep, and that the net addition they make to the national dividend is nil.

We have tried to estimate the value of their product by two methods—a direct and an indirect method. On the basis of personal discussions with the Professor of Agriculture at the Poona College and information obtained from publications of the "All India Cow Conference," we have obtained average figures of

TABLE 32

(In thousands)

	1925-26.	1929-30.	Difference.
Bulls	53,02	46,40	− 6,62
Bullocks	4,58,35	4,73,71	+ 15,36
Cows	3,79,01	3,87,85	+ 8,84
Young stock (calves) .	3,13,14	3,21,88	+ 8,74
Male Buffaloes . .	54,33	55,78	+ 1,45
She-buffaloes . . .	1,42,05	1,47,85	+ 5,80
Young stock (buffalo calves)	1,08,42	1,12,83	+ 4,41
Sheep	2,32,01	2,55,40	+ 23,39
Goats	3,92,95	3,59,43	− 33,52

yield, and worked out a figure of value of their annual milk yield. This we have checked by a figure of value of estimated consumption worked out from published studies of milk consumption. And on the basis of these two figures we have framed our final estimates of the value of their annual yield of milk. We have been helped in our calculations by the reports of committees appointed a few years ago in several provinces to enquire into the problem of milk supply, and also by collections of family budgets presented to the Royal Commission on labour as supplementary evidence in response to a special questionnaire issued by that Commission.

Table 32, page 92, gives classified statistics of the number of cattle and of sheep and goats in 1925-26 and 1929-30, which is very convenient from our point of view as that is just the period we are discussing.

For the purposes of our period we shall take a mean of the two figures as representative. We shall now proceed to discuss the contribution which these animals make under the several heads specified above.

Labour in Cultivation.

We have made no attempt to evaluate separately this part of the annual income from cattle, as its value is contained in the value of agricultural produce. Estimating it separately will compel us to deduct it from the value of agricultural produce, which procedure not only involves additional labour but will introduce an unnecessary element of error in our individual figures.

Income from Milk and Milk Products.

During the period there were on an average 38 million cows and 15 million cow-buffaloes. When trying to estimate the milk yield of these animals, we must remember that cows in this country cannot be compared in importance with, e.g., the position they occupy in English rural economy. The cow in India, as is pointed out by Lt.-Col. Matson in the "Agricultural Journal of India (1922)," is kept mainly for bearing calves which can be reared for the plough, while buffaloes are kept for producing milk. Mr. Leake points out in the same Journal (1923), that a "very *small proportion*" (italics ours) of the 60 million adult female bovine stock produce milk. That supply is drawn only from animals which give more than enough milk to support their own offspring." Mr. Sampson, in his special report on a cattle survey of the Madras Presidency, remarks that, "In the Madras Presidency there are no really good milking breeds of cattle, for the simple reason that in the country districts, among the agricultural population, milk as such is seldom used as an article of diet." Mr. Nilananda Chatterjee, Hon. Secretary of the All India Cow Conference Association, points out, that "the cattle of the United Provinces, the Central Provinces and Central India are more noted for their capacity as draught animals rather than as copious milkers. . . . It is worth noting that in the Punjab, United Provinces and the Bombay Presidency, the cow is valued more as the potential mother of bullocks than as good milkers." Discussion with the Professor of Agriculture also confirms the same view-point that cows in this country are not good milkers, and in many provinces numbers of them don't yield any milk at all. Further confirmation is available from the fact that Mr. Z. R. Kothavalla found in his survey of milch cattle in Bombay city that 95 per cent. of them were buffaloes; while Dr. Mann, in a similar survey for the city of Poona, found 80 per cent.

of the cattle kept by Gavalas to consist of buffaloes, and the survey of the Madras Dairy Trade (1917) gave 60 as the corresponding percentage. At the same time, honourable mention must be made of such breeds of cows as the Hansi, the Hissar, the Multani and Montgomery and the Gir types, but these are not typical of the country. In a personal discussion, it was suggested to me by the Professor of Agriculture at Poona, that I should take 200 lbs. per year as the average milk yield of the cows in India, but to make allowance for all contingencies, we have applied a rate of 300 lbs. as the annual yield, and a rate of 1500 lbs. as the annual yield of cow buffaloes. On the basis of these figures, we get the following figures of yield :—

TABLE 33

	Lbs.	
Cows . .	1150,29,00,000	
Buffaloes . .	2174,25,00,000	
Total .	3324,54,00,000	or 33245 million lbs.

We must add to this the value of milk given by goats. The goat is used in many parts of the country for milking purposes and it is, in fact, known as the poor man's cow. The milk is of course very rarely sold. Assuming a milk yield of 75 lbs. per head per year, we get a yield of 28,21 million lbs. The total output of milk —cows, buffaloes' and goats'—therefore would be 36066 million lbs.

Another estimate can be obtained by applying the figures of average yield per head of milch cattle given after careful consideration by Mr. Chatterjee in his "The Condition of Cattle in India." Applying his figure of 2 pints a day for 7 months in the year, we get 22192 million pints or 27740 million lbs. as the annual output of milk. Adding to this 2821 million lbs. on account of goat's milk the total output of all milk would be 30561 million lbs.

We shall now try to frame another estimate on the basis of consumption. The following table gives figures of average daily consumption per head of population of several towns, the statistics being based on special studies by men like Dr. Mann, G. R. Blackwood and L. S. Joshi, etc.

TABLE 34

	Lbs.
Bombay	0·27
Calcutta	0·26
Delhi	0·23
Ahmedabad	0·24
Poona	0·21
Surat	0·36
Sholapur	0·13
Hubli	0·16

The figures refer to the decade 1911-21, but we can reasonably assume, that not much change, at least in the direction of greater consumption, has taken place. The usual rate of consumption thus appears to be about 0·24 lbs. per head. This, however, takes only liquid milk consumption into account. If we assume that two thirds as much more milk is consumed in the form of ghi, we get for our period an annual consumption of 38330 million lbs.

We can now compare our results obtained on the basis of these three different methods :—

TABLE 35

OUTPUT

	(In millions)
Basis I	360,66
„ II	305,61
„ III	383,30

The figures do not reveal a very close agreement; but the estimates obtained on Basis I and Basis III are fairly near each other. We may therefore adopt a figure of 370 millions as the annual output of milk during this period. At the rate of 12 lbs. to the rupee, this would mean a value of Rs. 308 crores.

Income from Meat.

It is almost impossible to obtain any reliable statistics for India of slaughter for meat. The Royal Commission on Agriculture pointed out this grave defect in Indian agricultural statistics, and requested the Government to get returns sent by all licensed slaughter-houses; no action has so far been taken on the suggestion. We are therefore compelled to adopt indirect means for evaluating the income due to meat.

In a study made for the Department of Industries of the Bombay Government by Mr. Y. R. Gaitonde on " Village Tanning Industry in the Bombay Presidency," we obtain statistics showing the number of animals slaughtered at the slaughter-houses in various towns in

7

the Bombay Presidency in 1926. A summary is given below :—

TABLE 36

Buffaloes	39,263
Bullocks	52,869
Cows	60,589
Buffalo calves	3,991
Cow calves	18,177
Total bovine cattle	172,000
Goats	1,858,896
Sheep	476,372
Total goats and sheep	2,200,000

The total number of bovine cattle in Bombay Presidency during the year 1925-26 was 10,805 thousands, while that of goats and sheep was 62,50 thousands. This give us as the average rate of cattle slaughtered to cattle in existence 1·6 per cent. while the corresponding figure for goats and sheep is 35 per cent. Assuming that the same rate can be applied to the cattle and goats and sheep in the rest of India, we get the following annual figures of slaughter :—

Cattle	23,64,000
Goats and sheep	216,96,000

Valuing the slaughtered cattle at an average figure of Rs. 10 per head, and that of goats and sheep at Rs. 7 (I am indebted for these figures to Professor Gangulee, Member, Royal Commission on Agriculture, with whom I had a discussion on this subject in London), we get the value of meat as Rs. 17,55,44 thousands or nearly Rs. 18 crores.

We shall now frame another estimate on the basis of consumption. The different railway administrations had to supply some family budgets of their workers to the Royal Commission on Labour, and these figures are classified by provinces. Among the items figure "fish and meat," and the average expenditure per family (4·5 persons) per month on this item is given in Table 37. We have given in the same table statistics of the total population of the provinces for which these figures are available in order that we may attach due weight to each figure in striking our figure of average consumption per family for the whole of British India.

TABLE 37

Province.	Value of Consumption of Fish and Meat Per Month.	Population of the Province (in Millions).
C.P.	0 3 6	15·5
U.P.	0 5 11	48·4
Bihar and Orissa . .	0 7 10	37·7
Bengal	0 13 9	50·1

The weighted figure of consumption per family comes to 8·7 annas per month.

From statistics of family budgets supplied by the Government of the Central Provinces to the Labour Commission, it appears that in the four principal towns of that Province, about 60 per cent. of the families consume meat and fish. This includes families who consume even a small amount. The percentage is not unreasonable when we remember that 30 per cent. of the population consist of Muslims and Christians, and that a good many Hindus are non-vegetarians. Applying the percentage to the whole of India, we get 34·7 million families as consuming fish and meat. The value of meat and fish consumption per year thus comes to Rs. 2264 lakhs or nearly Rs. 23 crores. When we consider that this figure of consumption is obviously greater than our figure because it includes fish, the remarkable closeness of these two estimates of the value of meat—one based on production, the other on consumption—becomes apparent. We may therefore place the value of meat produced in a year at Rs. 18 crores, and that of fish at Rs. 5 crores.

Income from Hides and Skins.

Statistics of output of hides and skins are not available, and we have to use an indirect method in order to estimate the value of this addition to the national income.

Mr. Gaitonde's report, already referred to, gives figures of the number of hides and skins available in Bombay Presidency as 15 lakhs and 43 lakhs respectively, and the value of these hides and skins is put by him at Rs. 2 crores. If we assume that what is true of the value of hides and skins from the livestock of Bombay also applies to that of the rest of India, and if we weight the hides at six times the value of skins (the hide usually weighs 18 lbs. as against 2 lbs. of the skin, but the value per lb. of skin is one and a half times that of the value per lb. of hide, hence the weight of six given to hides is appropriate), we get Rs. 2634 lakhs as the annual value of our output of hides and skins.

Our figure compares well with the figure of Rs. 22·5 crores which Professor Gangule advances in a note prepared by him on the subject. It may be noticed that the annual value of exports of hides and skins during our period was Rs. 24·5 crores. But a part of this is due to the additional value due to tanning (the value of the exports of tanned hides and skins was Rs. 8·2 crores) and a part due to exports from the hides and skins produced in Indian States. If we halve the figure of exports to represent the value of exports of raw hides and skins from British India (Rs. 8 crores for Indian States and Rs. 4 crores for the value of tanning), we would get the value of total production to be a little more than twice that of exports, i.e. the domestic consumption of raw hides and skins becomes a little more than export of the same, which is not improbable. We may therefore evaluate the contribution to the national income from hides and skins at Rs. 25 crores.

Income from Wool.

No statistics of yield or value are available and we have to frame an estimate. If we assume an average yield of 3 lbs. per sheep maintained, we get a total production of 73 million lbs. of raw wool. The quantity of exports during the period was on an average 49 million lbs. per year; of this, however, 23 million lbs. may be regarded as re-exports of wool imported by land. That leaves an export of 26 million lbs. from India, but this includes exports from the Indian States. The exports from British India may be considered to be 16 million lbs.; our figure of production is 73 million lbs., this gives a domestic consumption of raw wool which is somewhat more than three times the exports—which does not appear improbable. To be on the safe side, however, we shall make domestic consumption precisely three times that of exports; that gives us 64 million lbs. as the total production of raw wool in the country. Applying to this quantity a price per lb. which is only a little less than the value per lb. of raw wool exported in our period, we get Rs. 5 crores as the value of the annual output of raw wool in this country.

Income from Bones, Horns, Tips, etc.

No statistics are available of output or value. The figures of export are as under :—

TABLE 38

(In thousands of Rs.)

	1925-26.	1926-27.	1927-28.	1928-29.	1929-30.
Bones . .	8,916	9,776	9,764	9,492	10,821
Horns, tips, etc. .	935	791	918	796	753

This gives an average value of exports of bones at Rs. 9754 thousands and of horns, tips, etc., at 839 thousands.

The combined total is Rs. 106 lakhs. If we assume a domestic consumption of two and a half times the quantity of exports, we get the value of the production of bones, horns, tips, etc., to be Rs. 371 lakhs or nearly 4 crores.

Additions to Livestock.

During the quinquennial period 1925-28 to 1929-30 livestock in India recorded a general increase. Bullocks increased by 1536 thousands, cows by 884 thousands, calves by 874 thousands, buffaloes (male) by 145 thousands, (female) by 580 thousands, and calves by 441 thousands. There was a reduction in the number of bulls by 662 thousands. Sheep increased by 2339 thousands while goats fell by 3352 thousands. If we take the average value of bullocks at Rs. 50 a pair, of cows at Rs. 20 per head, of buffaloes at Rs. 40, of calves at Rs. 10, and sheep and goats at Rs. 7, we get the value of the increase during the quinquennial period as Rs. 724 lakhs. The value per year would then come to Rs. 182 lakhs or nearly Rs. 2 crores. This figure allows for the loss due to the diminution in the number of goats and of bulls. The value of the export of living animals during the same period came to Rs. 39 lakhs. If we make allowance for the fact that a part of this is attributable to Indian States, a part to the export of animals other than cattle, and a part to the higher values natural for bovine stock considered worthy of export, we get about Rs. 20 lakhs as the value of livestock exported from British

India. This would give us, on the basis of Rs. 2 crores being the value of increments to our livestock, an internal trade in living animals of about nine times that of exports—which again is not an improbable proportion. We may therefore accept Rs. 2 crores per year as the value of additions to our livestock.

Income from Manure.

The contribution which the livestock make in the form of manure is quite considerable. But most of this dung is used up in the soil and forms a part of the value of agricultural produce. If we add in this chapter the income due to manure, we shall later have to deduct it from the value of agricultural produce. We have therefore preferred not to add anything under this head when considering the income due to livestock.

Income from Horses, Mules, Donkeys, Camels, etc.

The number of these animals in 1925-26 and in 1929-30 is given below :—

TABLE 39

(In thousands)

	1925-26.	1929-30.
Horses . . .	753	755
Mares . . .	698	707
Young stock . .	233	240
Mules . . .	69	75
Donkeys . .	1408	1380
Camels . . .	506	526

The income due to these animals is mostly contained in the figures of income due to heads "Transport," "Trade" and "Industry," and if we count it in here, we will have to deduct it there. It is therefore best not to add anything to our figure specifically as income due to these animals.

Conclusion.

We are now in a position to frame our estimate of the annual addition which livestock make to the national income. This is made up of the following items :—

TABLE 40

	(In lakhs of Rs.)
Labour in cultivation . .	Not added
Milk and milk products . .	308,00
Meat	18,00
Hides and skins . . .	25,00
Wool	5,00
Bones, horns, tips, etc. . .	4,00
Additions to livestock . .	2,00
Manure	Not added
Horses, mules, donkeys, etc. .	Not added
Total .	362,00

The contribution of livestock excepting for the items noted above thus comes to Rs. 362 crores. To this we may add Rs. 5 crores as the income due to fishing on the basis of consumption statistics. If we add another

Rs. 2 crores as the income due to hunting, we get a total of Rs. 369 crores as the income due to "Exploitation of Animals." [1]

[1] It must not be forgotten that this does not represent the total value of the income due to livestock, if we were considering livestock in isolation ; for then we will have to add the income due to their labours in cultivation and their supply of manure which would be very considerable indeed. It is only because we are considering the national income *as a whole* that we could afford to neglect these two very important items when dealing with the value of the produce from livestock.

CHAPTER VI

EXPLOITATION OF ANIMALS AND VEGETATION—FORESTS

THERE are fairly complete statistics regarding forests. Forests form a provincial subject, but there is an annual publication on " Statistics of Forest Administration in British India," and as fortunately in this country practically all forests are State-owned and income from them form an addition to State revenues, we can get a fairly accurate idea of the total income due to forest produce.

The following table gives statistics of area, output and value of forest produce during the period we have selected for study :—

TABLE 40(*a*)

(In thousands)

	Area Sq. Miles.	Outturn of Timber and Fuel, Cubic Feet.	Minor Produce	Gross Revenue of Govt.
1925-26 . .	228	410,617	1,43,12	5,98,71
1926-27 . .	227	362,035	1,35,88	6,19,65
1927-28 . .	250	370,174	1,43,15	6,13,09
1928-29 . .	250	389,928	1,51,78	5,78,09
1929-30 . .	250	350,067	1,50,84	6,13,22

This gives an average value of Rs. 605 lakhs as the annual value of forest produce. To this, however, must be added Rs. 68 lakhs, which is the average value of the produce given away free or at reduced rates. That gives us a total of Rs. 673 lakhs, or nearly Rs. 7 crores.

When we refer to the figures of valuation (at port of shipment) of exports of forest produce, we find a large discrepancy.

TABLE 41

Export of Forest Produce.

	(In thousands of Rs.)
1925-26	12,84,98
1926-27	10,83,30
1927-28	12,73,47
1928-29	13,49,24
1929-30	11,66,45

This gives an average of Rs. 1231 lakhs as the value of exports, and cannot be explained away on the ground that exports are also from the produce of Indian States. On examining the figures of exports, we find that the chief item is lac which was exported to a value of Rs. 7 crores during the period, and this does not figure in the items which constitute the output of forest produce. Adding this figure to that of the value of output as given in the Forest Administration Statistics, we get Rs. 14 crores. To this may be added 10 per cent. to represent the value of domestic consumption of lac of the produce of private forests, etc., and we then get Rs. 15·4 crores as the value of the addition which forests make to the national income.

We are now in a position to determine the contribution of the head "Exploitation of Animals and Vegetation" to the National Income. This comes to Rs. 1674 crores, being made up as under :—

TABLE 42

	(In crores of Rs.)
Agriculture	1289·6
Livestock	362·0
Fishing and hunting	7·0
Forests	15·4

And this 1674 crores of rupees represents the annual contribution of 83·2 million persons. But it must not be forgotten that this figure is a gross figure, and no deductions have so far been made for that part of the cost of production which is not available for human consumption (except certain items of the income from livestock, such as value of labour in cultivation and of manure).

Chapter VII

EXPLOITATION OF MINERALS

Compared to the size and population of the country, our mineral resources cannot be described to be particularly great. Our chief minerals are coal and petroleum (gold figures largely in the output of minerals from Indian States), with manganese, iron ore, lead, salt, and silver following at a distance.

Statistics of output and of value are fairly complete, but when considering the comparability of the value figures with that of other countries, we must remember that our figures are subject to considerable qualifications. As Mr. J. C. Brown points out in his "India's Mineral Wealth," "The value of coal represents an approximate pit's mouth figure, which bears little relation to the selling price in the open market. The value of salt is exclusive of its duty, the export value of mica is not connected in any apparent way with the stated value of the production figures at the mines." These defects do not affect the validity of the figures for our purpose, for we are considering here only the addition to the national income due to minerals. The income due to trade in the minerals, that due to the salt duty and that due to manufacture will all figure in the income due to trade, cost of government and industry.

We can now proceed to a brief survey of the principal Indian minerals.

Coal.

Coal is found mainly in Bihar and Orissa and in some parts of Bengal. The two well-known coal-fields are the Raniganj and the Jharia coal-fields. The production of coal has been showing a steady increase, culminating in a stage when schemes for restriction of output have begun to be discussed. We are in a position to meet our home demands almost entirely by domestic production, and in addition we have an export trade which is still an important source of demand. The following table gives figures of output and value of coal during the period 1925-29 :—

TABLE 43

(In thousands)

	1925.	1926.	1927.	1928.	1929.
Output (tons) .	19,969	21,093	21,019	21,516	22,308
Value (Rs.) .	12,10,35	9,73,02	9,02,40	8,40,06	8,48,40

The figures clearly reveal the gradual tendency to over-production leading to a fall in the absolute values, in spite of an increase in output. The annual average value of coal in our period is thus Rs. 955 lakhs.

Petroleum.

Petroleum is found mostly in Burma. There are also certain oil springs in Assam, the Punjab, and in the Kohat district and Shiram hills of the North-West Frontier Province. More than 95 per cent. of the production, however, is in Burma and is controlled by one powerful company, viz. the Burma Oil Corporation. There is a large demand for petrol in this country, and in recent years not only have exports almost ceased, but imports have had to supplement domestic production. There is, however, a considerable export of petroleum products like paraffin, wax and candles. The following table gives figures of output and value of petroleum mined in British India :—

TABLE 44

(In thousands)

	1925.	1926.	1927.	1928.	1929.
Output (gallons)	289,607	280,369	281,114	305,944	306,148
Value (Rs.)	10,29,52	978,94	592,48	578,10	643,26

The annual value of petroleum during our period thus comes to Rs. 764 lakhs.

Manganese Ore.

Manganese is an important mineral as the development of the Bessemer and open-hearth processes for making steel involve a very heavy use of manganese ores by the steel industry, and at least 90 per cent. of the world's output of this mineral is used for these processes. It is also used in the heavy chemical, electrical and glass industries. Manganese is found largely in the Central Provinces, Central India, the Vizagapatam district of Madras, and some parts of the Bombay Presidency. India is the largest single producer of this mineral, most of which she exports. The following table gives figures of output and value :—

TABLE 45

(In thousands)

	1925.	1926.	1927.	1928.	1929.
Output (in tons) .	710	857	879	717	751
Value (in Rs.) .	2,96,81	2,94,58	3,05,43	2,38,24	1,78,81

The annual value of manganese ore during our period comes to Rs. 263 lakhs.

Lead, Zinc and Silver.

Although lead has been found in a large number of places in India, the rise and development of the lead, zinc and silver industries of India are all associated with the opening up of the great ore deposit of Bawdin in the Northern Shan States in Burma. As a matter of fact, with the exception of a small supply of silver from Madras, the entire output of Indian lead, zinc and silver ore are from the province of Burma. The following tables give figures of output and value in our period :—

TABLE 46

OUTPUT

(In thousands)

	1925.	1926.	1927.	1928.	1929.
Lead (in tons) .	47	54	66	78	80
Silver (ounces) .	4,832	5,104	6,005	7,405	7,281
Zinc (in tons) .	21	43	67	76	67

TABLE 47

VALUE

(In thousands of Rs.)

	1925.	1926.	1927.	1928.	1929.
Lead . .	2,21,07	2,25,95	2,20,28	2,22,05	2,50,00
Silver .	93,37	88,50	94,67	1,19,26	1,07,31
Zinc . .	20,80	43,04	70,06	74,11	68,61
Total . .	3,35,24	3,57,49	3,85,01	4,15,42	4,25,92

The annual value of our output of lead, zinc and silver thus comes to Rs. 384 lakhs.

Salt.[1]

The production of salt in India is not sufficient for domestic consumption, about a fifth of which is met

[1] I may point out that for a good deal of the descriptive material of this chapter I am indebted to Mr. J. C. Brown's "India's Mineral Wealth."

by imported salt. 60 per cent. of Indian salt is derived from the evaporation of sea water carried on during the hot weather on the coasts of Bombay, Madras and Burma; salt is also made from sub-soil and lake brines, especially in the desert region of Rajputana, to the tune of nearly 250 thousand tons. About a tenth of the output comes from the rock salt mines of Kohat and of Mandi State. The production of salt is in this country a State monopoly, and Government levy their duty at the source. The following table gives statistics of output and value :—

TABLE 48

(In thousands)

	1925.	1926.	1927.	1928.	1929.
Output (in tons) .	1295	1639	1612	1515	1709
Value (in Rs.) .	76,35	1,12,04	1,13,57	99,92	1,13,14

The annual value of salt production thus comes to Rs. 103 lakhs.

Iron Ore.

It is well known that knowledge of iron metallurgy in India dates back to very ancient times, and till the advent of imported metal, the native iron industry was both widespread and prosperous. Attempt at manufacturing iron in this country on a modern basis, however, took a long time to succeed, and it was not till the Bengal Iron & Steel Co., and the Tata Iron & Steel Co., came on the scene that the modern Indian iron industry came into existence. War and protection have sustained the impetus which led to its development, and the output of iron ore nearly trebled itself during the period 1925-29. More than 90 per cent. of the output is from the huge deposits of Singhbhum in Bihar and Orissa. Burma and the Central Provinces have the small outputs of 50 and 1 thousand tons respectively. The following table gives figures of output and value :—

TABLE 49

(In thousands)

	1925.	1926.	1927.	1928.	1929.
Output (in tons) .	531	602	1070	1208	1437
Value in Rs. .	14,52	14,85	27,86	30,02	33,50

The annual value of iron ore comes on an average to Rs. 24 lakhs.

Copper Ore.

Copper ores, again, have been smelted in India since the days of antiquity and minerals containing copper have been found in every province, but deposits of a commercial value are found chiefly in Bihar and Orissa and to some extent in Burma. The following table gives figures of output and value :—

TABLE 50

(In thousands)

	1925.	1926.	1927.	1928.	1929.
Output (in tons) .	34	21	17	29	88
Value (in Rs.) .	40,15	46,68	45,14	49,88	64,79

The annual value of copper ore mined in India works out at Rs. 49 lakhs.

Zinc.

The most important source is at Bawdin in Burma where it is found along with lead, silver and copper minerals. There is a large domestic consumption of zinc and our resources are sufficient, in Mr. Brown's opinion, to make us a very important factor in the world's supply in course of time. The following table gives figures of output and value :—

TABLE 51

(In thousands)

	1925.	1926.	1927.	1928.	1929.
Output (in tons) .	21	43	67	76	67
Value (in Rs.) .	20,80	43,04	70,06	74,11	68,01

The annual value of zinc ore thus comes to Rs. 45 lakhs.

Other Minerals.

Among other minerals must be mentioned mica, in which we have nearly a monopoly of the world's supply. The following table gives statistics of value of other minerals for which figures are available :—

TABLE 52

(In thousands of Rs.)

	1925.	1926.	1927.	1928.	1929.
Mica . .	21,73	21,99	24,27	23,94	26,51
Tin ore . .	35,63	44,30	50,35	45,41	54,09
Wolfram .	4,52	7,71	5,70	3,00	15,17
Saltpetre .	19,00	13,00	15,00	9,80	9,40
Magnesite .	4,15	3,42	2,03	1,42	1,09
Chromite .	3,35	2,55	2,67	2,74	3,35
Jadestone .	1,63	4,70	3,02	5,82	4,86
Rubies . .	3,65	4,67	2,80	1,78	1,82
Gold . .	21	73	1,44	8	—
Total .	93,87	103,07	107,28	93,99	116,29

These do not cover the entire output of minerals in the country. There are a number of other minor minerals, such as limestone, stone, latente, bauxite, steatite, apatite, kyanite, etc. ; we may roughly estimate the value of their output at 5 per cent. of the value of the major minerals and others for which we have statistics of value. This gives us a figure of Rs. 135 lakhs.

We are now in a position to estimate the annual value of the output of minerals in this country.

TABLE 53

	(In lakhs of Rs.)
Coal	955
Petroleum	764
Manganese ore	263
Lead, zinc and silver	384
Salt	103
Iron ore	24
Copper ore	49
Zinc	45
Other minerals	103
	26,90
Add 5 per cent. to cover value of minerals for which statistics of value are not available	135
Total	28,25

The income due to "Exploitation of Minerals" is thus a little more than Rs. 28 crores, and accounts for 251 thousand incomes.[1]

[1] This figure is a little less than the more accurate figure which we obtain from the returns of men employed in mines; but we prefer to use the census figure in order to preserve the consistency of our thesis.

Chapter VIII

INDUSTRY

The contribution of industries to the national dividend is very difficult to measure with any precision. Statistics of output are only available for the jute and cotton industries; for the other organised or factory industries we get figures of number of establishments and of men employed; for the small industries—which predominate, at least so far as members employed by them are concerned—there are no statistics at all besides what we obtain of the number of workers under different occupational heads.

We have employed the method of valuation of the average income of the worker in the small industries and proceeded to build up an estimate of the contribution they make to the national income on that basis. For the most important class of workers employed in small industries, viz. handloom weavers and other textile workers, we have figures of production of handloom cloth, and we can build up an estimate of the value of their output. For barbers and washermen, who, between them, form the next most important class, we have obtained a value of the annual output of their services on the basis of consumption statistics and family budgets for a number of provinces which were specially prepared by the Railway Administrations and several provincial governments for submission as evidence before the Royal Commission on Labour. For the remaining number of workers employed in small industries, who form about two-thirds of the total number, we have obtained an average income per head by multiplying which with the number of workers we get a figure of the value of their annual income, which is the same thing as the value of their output. We have based this figure on a survey of some wage statistics available for the provinces of Madras and the Punjab, but more particularly on the basis of memoranda supplied by the different provincial governments on the unregistered factories of each province. These memoranda contain some figures of monthly earnings of different classes of workers. On the basis of these figures and bearing in mind the varying degree of their importance by different provinces, we have fixed up a figure of average income per head. Our figure gains importance from the fact that studies of urban workers undertaken in one province give an average very near ours, and the reasonableness of our estimate is established when we compare the value of industrial output thus arrived at with that of agricultural produce.

We must claim that our method leads to a more reasonable result than is obtained by the procedure hitherto followed by either adding a percentage to the value of agricultural produce or of summing up a number of guesses at the contribution of each type of industry. Moreover, since we are concerned only with the net increment to value made by industry, our method is likely to lead to a much smaller margin of error. In view of the nature of our small industries and the type of fixed capital employed, it is a reasonable assumption to make that the net value of our industrial output is equal to the sum of the value of the raw material and that of the labour employed in transforming it. No statistics of the amount or value of the raw material employed by each industry are available, and if we were to estimate the contribution of small industries by other than the "income method"—I may add that the "income method" is employed by Mr. Clark in his "National Income" of Great Britain to estimate the value of certain incomes which do not come under income tax statistics—we would have to estimate the value of raw material in order to deduct it from the value of industrial produce, as otherwise there will be double counting, and this would lead to an unnecessary source of error. These details would have become necessary if we were employed in discussing only the position of small industries. But we are concerned with the compilation of the national income, and so long as there is no double counting on the whole, there is no need to have guess work and net figures for each item. Finding net figures under each head would lead to a search for the items to be deducted under each head, with a resulting multiple possibility of error. We have, therefore, left the subject of deductions to a separate chapter, where we shall link it up with the national income as a whole and not its individual constituents.

As regards the income contributed by the organised industries, we have figures of output for the cotton and jute industries, and we have applied wholesale prices in valuing their output. For a number of others, we get useful statistics in the reports and appendices of particular Tariff Boards. As regards the rest—which employ about less than half of the total number employed—we have had to attempt an estimate which is of a less accurate character. We shall first discuss the value of the output of organised industries, and then proceed to that of small industries.

Large Industries.

The following table gives biennial figures of the number of men employed under the several groups which make up what are known as "Large Industrial Establishments":—

TABLE 54

(In thousands)

	1925.	1927.	1929.	1931.
Engineering . .	244,564	256,361	253,699	210,646
Textiles . . .	689,674	689,840	700,066	653,028
Minerals and metals .	59,087	55,830	54,924	47,352
Food, drink and tobacco . .	163,107	173,573	180,759	173,578
Chemicals, dyes, etc. .	40,282	47,938	48,546	47,204
Paper and printing .	39,729	41,480	44,741	42,642
Processes *re* wood and stone . . .	39,502	41,129	41,347	35,443
Processes *re* hides and skins . . .	6,118	5,802	6,211	5,030
Gins and presses . .	174,033	176,853	176,316	154,815
Miscellaneous . .	32,934	35,659	35,564	30,895
Total .	1,489,030	1,524,465	1,542,173	1,400,003

Textiles.

The two main items which make up this head are "cotton" and "jute."

The cotton manufacturing industry is the oldest and the most important of organised Indian industries. It gives employment to more than 350 thousand persons and there are about 270 joint stock companies with a paid up capital of Rs. 36 crores which are engaged in working the industry. The following table gives consolidated figures of the output of yarn and cloth :—

TABLE 55

(In thousands)

	1925-26.	1926-27.	1927-28.	1928-29.	1929-30.
Yarn (in lbs.) .	623,371	734,224	724,588	557,675	730,819
Cloth (in lbs.) .	416,783	487,198	509,293	376,513	484,621

We have decided to take the value figures only of cloth, as some of the yarn is consumed by the mills themselves and become a part of the cost of production of mill-coth, while a part is consumed by handlooms and goes into the cost of production of handwoven cloth. We shall, of course, add to the figure of value that we arrive at the value of our exports of yarn, and we will have to deduct—from the value of the entire domestic supply of cloth, both mill-made and hand-made—the value of the yarn that we import. The value of mill-made cloth during our period is roughly as follows :—[1]

TABLE 56

(In thousands of Rs.)

	1925-26.	1926-27.	1927-28.	1928-29.	1929-30.
Value of mill-made cloth .	56,31,19	53,45,98	56,19,46	44,24,32	52,77,71
Value of exports of yarn . .	2,93,37	3,08,54	1,87,91	1,95,67	1,90,24
Total .	59,24,56	56,54,52	58,07,37	46,19,99	54,67,95

From this we have to deduct the value of the raw cotton consumed by the industry in order to find out the industry's net increment of value. The following tables give the relevant figures :—

TABLE 57

(In thousands)

	1925.	1926.	1927.	1928.	1929.
Consumption (in bales of 400 lbs.)	2175	1983	2044	1765	1992
Value (Rs.) .	36,54,90	28,74,85	35,39,13	25,26,16	22,44,83

[1] My figures have been calculated after consultation with the secretary of the Bombay Millowner's Association, who was good enough to go through my statement and suggest corr ections.

The net increment value of the organised cotton industry is thus on an average Rs. 2527 lakhs. But it must be remembered that this figure excludes the value of the yarn which the mills sell as yarn in the domestic market, and it must further be remembered that our value figures are somewhat of an underestimate, as we have not made allowance for the variety of the items that constitute the mill industry's products.

Jute.

The jute industry is, as is well known, only next in importance and is almost exclusively located in the province of Bengal. It gives employment to 343,000 persons, and there are 77 mills with a paid-up capital of more than Rs. 16 crores. The steady progress of the industry is seen in the growth of the number of spindles and looms, which increased from 870 and 42 thousands to 1140 and 54 thousands respectively. No statistics of the value of production are available. From the report of the Indian Jute Mills Association, however, we get statistics of jute manufacture as also clearance of jute to Bombay, Karachi, Madras and also for local and up-country consumption. From these figures and the figure of exports we can compile two sets of figures of the output of jute manufactures. These two figures do not completely agree and we have preferred to adopt the figures of the output of jute manufactures which we obtain from the Report of the Indian Jute Mills Association. For the value, we have taken as our basis the declared value per unit of exported jute as most of our jute manufactures are exported. The following tables give the relevant figures :—

TABLE 58

(In lakhs)

	Output.		Value (Rs.).		
	Gunny bags (No.).	Cloth (yds.).	Gunny bags.	Cloth.	Total.
1925 . .	5153	15034	32,47	32,89	65,36
1926 . .	4988	15051	27,02	28,22	55,44
1927 . .	5132	15221	25,66	29,73	55,39
1928 . .	5857	15912	29,28	32,32	61,60
1929 . .	5937	16787	25,05	30,60	55,65

From this, however, we have to deduct the value of the raw jute consumed by the jute mills in order to get the net increment to value made by their output. We have obtained statistics of jute consumption from the Report of the Jute Mills Association, and we have worked out their values from our figures of value (*vide* Chapter IV).

TABLE 59

(In lakhs)

	Quantity of raw jute consumed (bales of 400 lbs.).	Value of figure in column 2.	Net value of jute manufactures.
1925 . .	53·4	49·25	16,11
1926 . .	53·7	22·38	33,06
1927 . .	56·3	23·11	32,28
1928 . .	58·8	26·13	35,47
1929 . .	62·5	23·81	31,84

The annual net value of jute manufactures therefore comes to Rs. 29,75 lakhs.

Paper Mills, Woollen Mills, etc.

Paper.—Statistics of output and value are available for the 8 paper mills, and are given below :—

TABLE 60

(In thousands)

	Quantity (tons).	Value (Rs.).
1925 . .	28	1,40,73
1926 . .	32	1,57,16
1927 . .	34	1,64,19
1928 . .	38	1,81,94
1929 . .	41	1,86,76

The average value of paper production thus comes to Rs. 166 lakhs.

Wool.—There are 12 woollen mills with a total paid-up capital of Rs. 130 lakhs. The total number of spindles and looms are on an average 82,000 and 1810 respectively, and the industry gave employment to nearly 7000 persons. The total raw wool available for consumption (including imports and deducting exports) is about 54 million lbs., valued at Rs. 4,25 lakhs. If we assume that the increment of value added by manufacture is 25 per cent., that gives us Rs. 106 lakhs as the value of the output of the woollen industry.

Heavy Chemicals.

In the Tariff Board Report on Heavy Chemicals, we get certain figures of local production of salt. They show a total of 3940 tons of salt of all kinds,[1] as against an import of 13,421 tons of salt. The import figures show a value of about Rs. 250 lakhs under the head "chemicals." We may therefore assign a value of Rs. 80 lakhs to the annual output of Indian Chemicals in our period.

Matches.

The Tariff Board Report on matches provides some useful statistics *re* the output of matches in India. In 1926 the total stock capital of the concerns engaged in match production was Rs. 117 lakhs, while the working capital amounted to Rs. 65 lakhs. The total capacity was 18·5 millions gross, while the actual production was 10·7 millions. During the same year the country imported 7·9 millions gross valued at Rs. 93 lakhs; in 1926-27 and 1927-28 the corresponding figures were

[1] Details are as under :—

TABLE 61

Glauber's salts	300	tons
Sodium sulphide . . .	nil	
Zinc chloride	nil	
Epsom salts	582	,,
Copperas	958	,,
Copper sulphate . . .	35	,,
Aluminium sulphate . .	1465	,,
Alum	600	,,
Total .	3940	

6·1 millions gross valued at Rs. 75 lakhs, and 3·3 millions gross valued at Rs. 44 lakhs respectively. We may accordingly value the annual match production during our period at about Rs. 120 lakhs.

Sugar.

The Tariff Board Report on sugar gives quite an elaborate discussion of the problem of assuring a

TABLE 62

(In thousands)

	1925-26.	1926-27.	1927-28.	1928-29.	1929-30.
Output of white sugar (tons) .	52	59	68	69	90
Quantity of cane consumed (tons)	642	694	791	803	990
Value of white sugar (Rs.) .	1,41,96	1,61,07	1,85,64	1,88,37	2,45,70
Value of cane consumed . .	1,25,00	1,20,00	1,27,00	1,40,00	1,71,00
Net increment of value by sugar manufacture .	16,96	41,07	58,64	48,37	74,70

domestic supply of sugar to this country. We get statistics of the output of white sugar from factories during the years 1925-26, and we also get an idea of the extent of sugar cane which is used for manufacture into white sugar. We have valued the white sugar at the rates given in the Tariff Board which works out on an average to Rs. 10 a maund; it may be noted that the percentage of extraction from the cane showed a consistent improvement in our period, rising from 8·07 per cent. to 9·07 per cent., with the result that the amount of cane consumed per ton of white sugar shows a steady fall. Table 62, page 135, gives figures of output, raw material consumed and net increment of value.

The net value of the annual output of white sugar thus comes to Rs. 48 lakhs.

Electric Wires and Cables.

The Tariff Board in considering the claims of the Indian Cable Co. for protection gives statistics of the value of this material produced in this country. Details are as under :—

TABLE 63

(Value in lakhs of Rs.)

	Domestic production.	Imports.
Rubber insulated cables . . .	9·7	36·9
Bare copper wire other than telegraphic and telephone wire . .	3·1	21·9
Telegraph and telephone wires and cables	6·6	2·9

The annual output thus comes to a value of about Rs. 20 lakhs.

We are in a position to set forth below the contributions of those parts of the organised industries for which figures of net values are calculable :—

TABLE 64

(Value in lakhs of Rs.)

Description.	No. of men employed.	Value.
Cotton mills [1]	350	15,86
Jute mills	343	29,75
Woollen mills	7	1,06
Paper mills	5	1,66
Match works	14	1,20
Chemicals	3	80
Electrical engineering	5	20
Sugar	14	48
Total	741	51,01

We must further exclude, as having already had their incomes counted, the 2000 persons employed in the preparation of lac and the 62,000 persons employed in the manufacture of tea. There thus remains 713,000 persons employed in the organised industries for which we have no statistics of output or value. This is nearly 100,000 less than the number for whose industries we have found an annual value of Rs. 51 crores. Considering the fact that the remaining industries are much less valuable (of gins, and presses, flour mills, rice mills, etc.), and also that they give employment to a number which is only about 90 per cent. of that given employment by the industries specified on the previous page, we may hazard a

[1] It must not be forgotten that the figure of net increment of value by cotton mills excludes the value of yarn *sold* by them, but consumed by Indian handlooms.

guess at the net value of their product to be Rs. 25 crores. Thus the annual value of the output of organised or factory industries in our period comes to Rs. 76 crores.

Small Industries.

We have already pointed out that no statistics of value or output are available for the output of these small industries (including the unregistered factories) which give employment to 104 lakhs of persons or nearly 87 per cent. of the total number of workers engaged in industry. We give below the figures we have worked out showing the average distribution of the 119 lakhs supported by industry during the period 1925-29.

TABLE 65

	(In thousands)
Textiles	3124
Hides, skins, etc.	200
Wood	1212
Metals	525
Ceramics	773
Chemicals	482
Food industries	1323
Industries of dress and toilet	2517
Furniture	14
Building	516
Construction of means of transport	22
Production of physical forces	15
Others	1197
Total	119,20

Of these, 1518 thousand persons are employed in the large industries, the value of the product of which has already been estimated. Deducting this figure we get 1,03,92 thousands as the figure of the number of incomes which make up the value of the output of small industries. Of these, again, there are some types of incomes for which we can build up estimates of value without resorting to the "average income method." Thus, e.g., we have got figures of production of the handloom weaving industry. During the period in question the production of cotton cloth by this section of the textile industry was 1231 million lbs. Assuming a value of Rs. 0-6-0 per yard (which is equal to the value per yard of coloured piece goods), we get the value of cloth woven by handlooms as Rs. 46,20 lakhs. We do not need to deduct from this figure the value of this industry's consumption of domestic yarn, as we have not included separately the value of any part of the domestic production of yarn in the compilation of our figure of national income. But we have not deducted the value of either the imports of raw cotton or of foreign yarn that we import from the figure of the value of mill-made cloth. This deduction will be made generally from the national income when we come to consider the deductions that we must make from the dividend before we can look on it as available for distribution and consumption by the people. To the figure of Rs. 46,20 lakhs we must add Rs. 7,19 lakhs as the value of silk goods produced on handlooms, which figure we obtain from the report of the Tariff Board on the sericultural industry in India. From the value of the silk goods we need not deduct the value of Indian raw silk as we had not previously included this item in our calculations, but more than 60 per cent. of the raw silk comes from abroad and its value has to be deducted. This comes to about Rs. 1,25 lakhs, thus leaving us with a net figure of Rs. 5,94 lakhs. We may add Rs. 1,00 lakhs to cover the net value of carpets, rugs and other hand-woven woollen goods. We now get against the 2441 thousand persons who obtain their living from handloom weaving and other textile operations unconnected with the use of machinery an income of Rs. 53,14 lakhs or a little more than Rs. 53 crores. That this figure is a fairly reasonable approximation to the real state of affairs becomes evident when we find that on this basis the average weaver's income comes to less than Rs. 2,18 per year—which is not inconsistent with the observed economic condition of the Indian weaver (particularly when we also note that the figure for the principal worker must be larger, as our average includes working dependants who perhaps figure most in this section of industry).

Then again, for two sub-heads—viz. barbers, and those engaged in washing and cleaning—which figure under the head " Industries connected with Dress and Toilet," we have some consumption statistics which may be used as a basis for valuing their incomes. We give below figures of monthly expenditure on the service of barbers and dhobies by families with small incomes (generally below Rs. 30 a month) in several provinces. We have compiled these figures from the evidence before the Labour Commission previously referred to in the beginning of this chapter.

TABLE 66

(Monthly expenditure by family)

	Barbers' services.	Dhobies' services.
United provinces [1] . .	Rs. 0 4 1	Rs. 0 5 3
Bihar and Orissa . .	" 0 3 5	" 0 4 1
Bengal	" 0 3 9	" 0 4 5
General average . . .	" 0 3 9	" 0 4 7
Yearly average . . .	" 2 13 0	" 3 7 0

These figures, however, refer only to expenditure in urban areas. In rural areas it is not unlikely that it may be even less than half of these figures. Assuming that rural monthly expenditure per family on dhobies and barbers is one half of that in towns, and weighting the figure in accordance with the proportion of rural to the total population, we get Rs. 1-9-0 and Rs. 1-14-0 as the national averages of the monthly expenditures per family on the services of barbers and dhobies respectively.

Applying these rates to the 603 lakhs of families in existence in the period under study, we get Rs. 942

[1] The averages for U.P. are based on two sets of figures ; one compiled from the budgets of all classes of workers in the three towns of Cawnpore, Lucknow and Gorakpur, viz. :—

	Cawnpore.	Lucknow	Gorakpur.
Barber	Rs. 0 4 9	Rs. 0 4 5	Rs. 0 3 11
Dhobi	" 0 6 9	" 0 4 9	" 0 5 10

and the other from the budgets furnished by the Railway Administration of that province.

lakhs as the annual value of barbers' services and Rs. 1131 lakhs as that of dhobies' services. Together, these account for the incomes of 15 lakhs of barbers and dhobies, giving them an average income of about Rs. 12 per month. This figure is, however, the national average. It will be much larger in the towns and a little smaller in the rural parts.

There now remain 6481 thousand workers whose incomes we have to evaluate. After a careful scrutiny of the data embodied in the evidence of different provincial governments before the Royal Commission on labour, and after taking into account the fact that a good many of the workers form a part of the village economy, and in so far as they perform services pertaining to the business aspect of the agriculturists' work their incomes are already included in the valuation of agricultural produce, we have decided to apply an average figure of Rs. 15 a month or of Rs. 180 a year as the income of the workers employed in the remaining small industries. This gives us Rs. 117,02 lakhs, or a little more than Rs. 117 crores as the net value of the output of the 6481 thousand workers engaged in the small industries other than handloom weaving and some of the industries connected with toilet and dress. Small industries, therefore, contribute to the national dividend an annual figure of Rs. 190,89 lakhs or Rs. 191 crores.

We are now in a position to evaluate the net output of all industry (excepting for the fact that deduction due to use of foreign cotton and yarn is not made in this chapter) as under :—

TABLE 67

	(In lakhs of Rs.)
Cotton mills	25,27
Jute mills	29,75
Woollen mills	1,06
Paper mills	1,66
Match factories	1,20
Chemicals	80
Electrical engineering	20
Sugar	48
Other organised industries	25,00
Total organised industries	76,01
Textiles (handlooms, etc)	53,14
Barbers	9,42
Dhobies	11,31
Other small industries	117,02
Total small industries	190,89
Grand total—all industries	266,90

This figure excludes the income of those engaged in the preparation of lac and of tea, as their incomes are already included in the chapter on valuation of agricultural produce.

We thus get very nearly Rs. 267 crores as the value of the output of the 119 lakhs of persons engaged in industry. Plausibility is lent to our figure when we consider that our calculations give us an average annual income of Rs. 224 per worker engaged in industry as against Rs. 196 per worker engaged in agriculture and dairying.

CHAPTER IX

TRANSPORT AND TRADE

TRANSPORT workers are classed under three heads, viz. Water Transport, Road Transport and Rail Transport. The figures which we have compiled are based on the census figures of 1921 and 1931 and are not quite representative of this particular period 1925-29 so far as workers on railways are concerned, because there was considerable retrenchment on the railways in 1930 and 1931.

Rail Transport.

During the period, the average gross value of the earnings of railways from the carriage of persons and goods was Rs. 103 crores. The interest paid on railways capital in England during the period was Rs. 12 crores; imports of railway plant and rolling stock came to Rs. 4 crores. If we take 50 per cent. of the earnings as paid in the shape of wages and salaries, we get the net contribution of railway services to be Rs. 43 crores. We have not followed the practice which has been followed in the " Wealth and Taxable Capacity of India " of treating the earnings of carrying passengers as " really only the expenditure of the travelling public," and therefore not necessary to be taken account of. The railways contribute to the national dividend not simply by their net profits, but by the value of the place-utility services they render minus that part of the cost which is not available for consumption in India and that which has been already counted in the evaluation of the other items in the national dividend. Our point is that the net contribution of railways is measured by the services of the labour and capital employed, and as our railways have mostly foreign capital, the contribution of railways may be treated as equivalent to their wages and salary bill.

Water Transport.

The total value of the coasting trade during the period (including both export and import) was Rs. 211 crores. If we assume that 5 per cent. of the total value be made up of the cost of transport, we get Rs. 10·5 crores as the value of the contribution of coastal water transport in India. To this we may add Rs. 105 lakhs to cover the value of such inland water transport as there is. Deducting 25 per cent. to cover repairs, depreciation, coal, etc., this gives us a figure of Rs. 9 crores as the value of the output of water transport services. Considering that there were 300,000 persons working on water transport during this period, this method would give Rs. 300 as the annual average income of each worker, including the higher paid workers.

Road Transport.

Road transport is a very comprehensive trade, as it includes the transport of goods and passengers by bullock carts both for purposes of pure road travel as well as for catching railways. The plying of means of conveyance in the principal towns is also included, as also the use of lorries and motor buses in the towns and all over the country, as also the use of trams. Only that part of the gross value of the output of such services is properly to be included which does not include the carriage of persons and goods the value of which has already been counted, and allowance has also to be made for that part of the cost which is not available for consumption within the country. The total value of the agricultural and industrial produce of the country in our period come to Rs. 1557 crores. To this may be added the Rs. 362 crores which forms the value of the income from livestock. It can reasonably be presumed that one half of the agricultural and livestock produce, and two thirds of the industrial produce, are transported by road over longer or shorter distances. As the length of the distance over which the goods are transported is smaller on an average than in the case of either rail or water transport, we may apply a flat rate of two per cent. to the value of the goods transported over road to represent the cost of the services of road transport. This gives us Rs. 20,08 lakhs as the value of the annual output of the services of road transport during the period. From this we may deduct 10 per cent. to cover the cost of repairs, depreciation, etc.; we are making no allowance here for the consumption of grain by the bullocks used for driving carts, because we are taking that into account in our chapter on "Deductions." We may deduct an additional 5 per cent. to allow for the extra cost incurred by the use of petrol by motor transport. This gives us Rs. 17 crores as the net value of the addition to the national income made by road transport. This figure compares reasonably with that of the output of railway services, and gives an average income of Rs. 203 per head to those engaged in road transport—which figure, again, is not improbable. We are now in a position to indicate the addition made by different classes of transport services, pointing out at the same time that our figures are less accurate than those of the other items we have calculated so far.

TABLE 68

	(In crores of Rs.)
Rail transport	43
Water transport	9
Road transport	17
	69

Trade.

No figures whatsoever are available of the earnings of traders, and the value of their services must be included in a computation of national income partly because we have taken figures of the harvest value of agricultural produce and partly because wholesale prices, on comparison with other prices, do not always contain an allowance for the value of transport and trade services, contrary to the assumption made in the "Wealth and Taxable Capacity of India." Half of the gross agricultural produce may be taken to be "traded," as also two-thirds of the industrial produce, and the whole of the forest and mineral produce.

In applying a percentage to the value of this produce to represent the net addition made to value by the services of trade, we have taken into account the difference between the domestic value and the value per exported unit of some of the Indian money crops. This would give a rate of more than 20 per cent. to represent the value of trade services, but the rate is swelled partly because the quality of the exported unit is uniformly superior, and partly because the trading expense of exported commodities are always greater. We have had also some personal discussions with several traders regarding the rate of their profits. Taking all relevant facts into consideration, we have decided to regard 10 per cent. as the average rate of profit on traded goods in this country, and applying this rate to the value of the traded produce, we get Rs. 100 crores as the annual value of the services of trade in our period. From this we may deduct 10 per cent. to cover cost of upkeep (other than wage and salary payments), depreciation, etc. This leaves the figure at Rs. 90 crores, which gives an income of Rs. 164 per worker engaged in trade—which is quite reasonable as compared with the figure of income received by workers engaged in industry, as our figure of people employed in commerce includes so many very small traders that we get a smaller *per capita* income for trade than for industry.

We can now sum up the net annual contribution of trade and transport to the national dividend as Rs. 159 crores, being made up of Rs. 90 crores on account of trade and of Rs. 69 crores on account of transport.

Chapter X

PUBLIC ADMINISTRATION, PROFESSIONS AND LIBERAL ARTS, AND DOMESTIC SERVANTS

The combined total of the number of persons employed under these two heads is 2682 thousands, of which public force and administration claim 1091 thousands.

Public Force and Administration.

Following Mr. Clark we have decided to include the cost of government in the valuation of the national dividend taken. The following table gives figures of that part of the governmental expenditure in this country which may properly be considered to be a part of the cost of government (both Central and Provincial).

TABLE 69

(In lakhs of Rs.)

	1925-26.	1926-27.	1927-28.	1928-29.	1929-30.
Civil administration .	59,88	62,07	63,14	65,59	68,13
Military services . .	60,39	60,92	56,34	58,49	59,08
Total .	1,20,27	1,22,98	1,19,48	1,24,09	1,27,21

The average figure comes to Rs. 1,22,81 lakhs per year.

From this we have to deduct the expenses incurred in England in connection with the performance of its functions by the Indian Government. This comes to £20·4[1] millions a year in our period, or Rs. 27,16 lakhs. Of the remaining Rs. 95,65 lakhs, 10 per cent. may be deducted to cover the cost of items which have already been counted in the valuation of the other factors that constitute the national income.

The profits on the posts and telegraph department ought also properly to be included, but as the item is negligible in amount we have not included it.

Professions and Liberal Arts.

No statistics of income or output of services are available. The All India Income Tax Reports give the following statistics of the income tax demand on " Professional Earnings " :—

[1] Details as under :—

TABLE 70

(In thousands of £)

1925-26 . . .	20,284
1926-27 . . .	20,147
1927-28 . . .	19,352
1928-29 . . .	20,198
1929-30 . . .	21,853
Average .	20,367

The figure includes expenditure in England on Civil Administration, Debt Services, Defence, Pensions and Allowances of both the Central and Provincial Governments.

TABLE 71

(In thousands of Rs.)

1925-26	30,91
1926-27	30,72
1927-28	31,62
1928-29	35,74
1929-30	34,89
Average figure for period . .	32,78

Assuming that the average rate of tax which this figure represents is nine pies in the rupee, we get Rs. 699 lakhs as the income of those followers of the professions and liberal arts who are assessed to income tax. The exception limit, however, is Rs. 2000 a year, and large numbers of the workers in the professions and liberal arts are thereby excluded. Moreover, the income tax figures do not represent quite accurately the facts regarding even those workers whose annual incomes exceed Rs. 2000 a year, as there is considerable evasion of tax under this head. We may, therefore, multiply this figure by 6 and we then get an income of Rs. 42 crores under this head. This gives an annual income of Rs. 280 per head to the worker engaged in professions and liberal arts, which is quite a reasonable figure.

Domestic Servants.

After careful consideration we have decided to take Rs. 10 a month as the average figure of the earnings of domestic servants per head in this country. This gives a figure of Rs. 60,30 lakhs as the contribution of domestic servants to the national dividend. We may deduct 10 per cent. from this figure to cover the output of the services of those of the domestic servants who are really engaged in attending on the business work of their employers, and whose incomes have therefore already been included in the valuation of agricultural and industrial produce. This leaves Rs. 53,77 lakhs or about Rs. 54 crores as the net annual value of the services of domestic servants.

We sum up below the results of this chapter :—

TABLE 72

	(In crores of Rs.)
Public force and administration .	86
Professions and liberals arts . .	33
Domestic servants . . .	54
Total .	173

Chapter XI

DEDUCTIONS

We shall consider in this chapter the various deductions to be made from our figures before we arrive at the net amount of the national income—the output of goods and services available for human consumption in this country.

Agriculture and Pasture.

We have to make an allowance for seeds, also for waste from exposure, deterioration, etc.

For a completely accurate figure of the amount needed for seeds, we must know the seed requirements of every crop and their variations by different provinces. It is very difficult to get these figures, and Mr. Mehta's [1] textbook of agriculture does not contain figures for more than a few crops. From the seed rates given there for jowar, bajri, wheat and rice, it appears that $2\frac{1}{2}$ per cent. would be a legitimate deduction that can be made on account of seed requirements. The rate that seems to have been adopted by Messrs. Shah and Khambhata mainly on the basis of Mr. Dubey's estimate is 2 per cent. The total value of agricul-

[1] "The Elements of Agriculture of the Bombay Presidency"—P. R. Mehta.

tural produce that is thus not available for human consumption on account of seed requirements is Rs. 31,65 lakhs.

We need make no deductions in respect of manure, and the draught power of the cattle employed in ploughing the land, as we have not included these items in our evaluation of the produce from livestock.

We have also to make an allowance for waste due to deterioration, exposure, insects, damp and forests, etc. Dr. Dubey puts this at 10 per cent. of the total output of agricultural produce. We may point out that this figure can satisfactorily be modified, and a more reasonable allowance would be about 7½ per cent. of the value of agricultural produce. This would come to Rs. 94,95 lakhs.

We have to deduct the value of the seeds consumed by bullocks; this we shall do along with the deduction we have to make for the consumption of grain by the milch cattle.

The total amount of the deductions to be made from the value of agricultural produce (except for the grain consumed by bullocks) comes to Rs. 127 crores, made up as under :—

TABLE 73

	(In lakhs of Rs.)
Seed	31,65
Waste	94,95
Total	126,60

The value of the grain consumed by the milch cows and buffaloes has to be deducted, as also that of the grain consumed by the draught cattle. We have been advised that hardly any grain is fed to cattle. Cows are almost completely neglected, while buffaloes and draught cattle in the ploughing season are fed with some oil seeds, oil cakes, grain, etc. We may adopt the following figures of annual consumption per head, viz. 750 lbs. of grain and seed for buffaloes, 50 lbs. for cows and 50 lbs. for bullocks. This gives a total consumption on the part of the bovine stock of 15,625 million lbs. of grain and seeds, which at a rate of 25 lbs. to the rupee gives 62,45 lakhs as the value of the item to be deducted on this account.[1]

We have to deduct 10 per cent. from the value of the output of minerals and forest produce to cover the cost of upkeep, depreciation, etc. This gives a figure of Rs. 4,37 lakhs.

We have also to allow for repairs, upkeep and depreciation of the fixed equipment employed in industry. The fixed equipment is important only in the case of large industries for which we may allow 10 per cent. on this account; for the small industry 2 per cent. would be quite a sufficient allowance. This makes the value of this item Rs. 12,02 lakhs.

No allowance need be made for raw material consumed by industry, as we have already made the necessary deductions in the case of the large industries, while

[1] Details are as under :—

51,574	thousand	bullocks and bulls at	50 lbs.—	258	million lbs.
14,495	,,	buffaloes at	750 ,, —	10,871	,, ,,
38,343	,,	cows at	50 ,, —	1,917	,, ,,

We may point out that our figures are supported by the general fact observed in dairy farms that half a lb. of grain is usually consumed for every lb. of milk produced.

in the case of small industries there is no need to do so (because we have estimated the value only of the services of the workers engaged in those industries).

No allowance need be made for repairs and depreciation under trade and transport as the necessary deductions have already been made when evaluating those items.

An allowance of only 1 per cent. may be made under professional incomes for costs of repairs and maintenance of office equipment, as many of the workers under this head have no fixed equipment of any character. This gives a figure of Rs. 42 lakhs to be deducted under this head.

In addition, we have to make deductions on account of the raw materials imported by this country and used up by our industry and agriculture. For the period selected this figure works out to an average of Rs. 27,32 lakhs, details of which are as under :—

TABLE 74

(In lakhs)

	1925-26.	1926-27.	1927-28.	1928-29.	1929-30.
Building and Engineering material . .	1,22	1,25	1,29	1,26	1,35
Coal	98	36	62	39	46
Raw cotton . .	3,64	5,03	6,74	3,90	3,42
Twist and yarn . .	7,77	6,62	6,79	6,29	6,00
Paper-making materials	26	35	40	42	45
Tea chests . . .	85	63	72	67	80
Metals (50 per cent.) .	9,03	8,38	10,71	10,12	8,60
Instruments and appliances . . .	3,54	4,01	4,47	4,92	5,38
Total .	27,29	22,63	31,74	27,97	26,46

We can now sum up the deductions to be made from the gross figure of the national income. This amounts to Rs. 233,18 lakhs or 233 crores, which is made up as under :—

TABLE 75

(In lakhs of Rs.)

On account of agriculture	126,60
,, livestock	62,45
,, minerals and forest produce	4,37
,, industry	12,02
,, professional earnings . .	42
,, import of raw materials .	27,32
Total .	233,18

Chapter XII

CONCLUSION

We are now in a position to evaluate the national income of British India. The gross income, allowing for certain deductions made in the course of our calculation of individual items, is Rs. 2301 crores, made up as under :—

TABLE 76

(In crores of Rs.)

Agriculture	1290
Livestock	362
Fishing and hunting	7
Forests	15
Minerals	28
Industry	267
Trade	90
Transport	69
Public force and administration	86
Professions	33
Domestic service	54
Grand total	2301

From this figure we have to deduct Rs. 233 crores, details of which have already been discussed in the previous chapter. The net figure of our national income is thus Rs. 2068 crores, and all the 1190 lakhs of incomes of which we were in quest during the course of our investigation have now been accounted for. The income *per capita* works out at Rs. 79·5.

But we have not made any allowance for the profits of private foreign capital in this country. We have worked out elsewhere (*Economic Journal*, March 1932) an estimate of the total amount of foreign capital in India at a little less than £600 millions. Of this, £330 millions formed the sterling debt of the Government of India. The amount of foreign capital invested in private firms and institutions is a little more than £250 millions. If we apply to this figure an average rate of profit of 8 per cent., we get £20 millions or Rs. 2670 lakhs as the profits of foreign capital in India and therefore not available for Indian consumption. We may also make an allowance of Rs. 18 crores to cover remittances abroad made by foreigners resident in the country. This gives us the real net figure of national income available for human consumption in India at Rs. 2023 crores. *On the basis of this figure, we get a per capita income of Rs. 77·9 or an annual income of Rs. 390 per family of five persons.*

The Per Capita Income.

Rs. 77·9 per head per year—a little more than 1 rupee a day for a family of five—surely these figures are enough to cause dismay to any well-wisher of India! They reveal an appalling condition of poverty and serve to explain the well-known phenomenon of the high Indian birthrate and the high Indian death-rate. Even a bare existence is possible at this range, simply because the vast majority of our population live in hovels, economise in clothes, know no furniture, rarely drink milk, hardly eat meat or fruits or other expensive though nutritious items of diet, and obtain little or no scope for expending on the "Miscellaneous"—that well-known item in the family budget which serves as an index of the level of the standard of life of the family.

The fact of Indian poverty becomes even more striking when we remember that Rs. 77·9 is an average that comprises the incomes of both the millionaire and the manual labourer. Unfortunately, no reliable statistics of distribution are available in this country. But if we assume that there are 700,000 cultivators, landlords, etc.—including zemindars of permanently settled estates whose income alone amounts to Rs. 31 crores—with an average of Rs. 2000 a year, and if we add to the 140 crores of rupees the Rs. 235 crores which is assessed to income tax and forms the non-agricultural income of 300,000 assessees with incomes of over Rs. 2000 a year, we get Rs. 375 crores as the income of a well-to-do class numbering 10,00,000. If we assume that the number of persons supported by each earner is 4 in this class, we get their total strength as 50,00,000. Deducting these figures from the totals for the entire population of British India, we get Rs. 64·6 as the *per capita* income of the vast mass of the people of this country.

Trend of Movement in the Per Capita Income.

We may now compare the figure we have worked out with some of the previous estimates which we have discussed in detail and amended in the light of our own investigations. In the following table we reproduce these estimates, along with figures showing what the *per capita* income in the different years mentioned would stand at, in terms of the price-levels of the five years 1925-29.

TABLE 77

Author.	Estimate.	Year referred to.	Change in price level.	Estimate at price levels of 1925-29.	Movement compared with our figure.	Period in years.
Dr. Naoroji .	23·5	1867-68	+ 88 per cent.	44·2	+ 75 per cent.	60
Atkinson .	31·5	1895	+ 75 per cent.	55·0	+ 40 per cent.	30
Shah and Khambhata .	88·0	1921-22	− 11 per cent.	78·0	Nil.	5

We must point out that, strictly speaking, these different figures are not comparable, as the basis of computation is not the same in all cases. Nevertheless, the figures reveal that India has not been growing poorer in an absolute sense; at the same time, they also reveal unmistakably that our pace of progress is very slow, the national income appears to increase by about 1 per cent. every year, and as the other civilised nations of the world have been progressing in production at a rapid rate, we are becoming poorer from a relative point of view. In relation to the rest of the world, we are worse off to-day than we were 60 years ago, and this fact explains to some extent the strength of feeling underlying the plea of India's growing poverty.

Provincial Distribution.

We might also notice that comparison of the provincial figures of agricultural income shows that, generally speaking, the different provinces have retained their position in the nation's agricultural economy. The following table speaks for itself :—[1]

TABLE 78

PERCENTAGE OF THE INCOME CONTRIBUTED BY THE AGRICULTURE OF EACH PROVINCE TO THE TOTAL INCOME OF ALL PROVINCES MENTIONED IN THE TABLE.

Province.	Naoroji.	Baring-Barbour.	Shah and Khambhata.	Findlay Shirras.
Bengal . .	34·7	32·5	31·6	31·7
N.W. provinces and Oudh . .	19·1	22·5	21·1	10·0
Madras . .	13·0	15·6	14·8	14·6
Punjab . .	13·0	10·6	9·8	13·0
Bombay . .	14·4	12·2	15·2	11·6
C.P. . . .	5·8	6·5	7·5	7·9

[1] The figures have been calculated by me from the works of the authors cited above. In the later works, North-West Provinces and Oudh give way to the United Provinces of Agra and Oudh ; while Bengal gets divided into Bihar and Orissa and Bengal.

We found, when compiling the percentages from the estimates of Messrs. Shah and Khambhata, that their table containing the details of the agricultural wealth of India by provinces contains serious mistakes of additions for Bombay, Sind and the Punjab ; and we have made the necessary alterations when framing this table.

The only changes common to all the different estimates appears to be in the case of Bengal, Madras and Central Provinces. Bengal has slightly deteriorated in her proportionate importance, while Madras and Central Provinces seem to have improved their position a little. Still, taking the table as a whole, there are no startling changes and there does not therefore appear to have been any significant alteration in the balance of provincial agricultural economics.

The National Income and the Burden of Taxation.

Before we conclude this essay we may work out the burden of taxation with reference to the national

TABLE 79

(In thousands of Rs.)

Items.	1925-26.	1926-27.	1927-28.	1928-29.	1929-30.
Customs .	47,77,95	47,38,11	48,21,42	49,28,01	51,27,66
Income tax .	16,12,04	15,98,29	15,42,64	17,05,65	17,06,35
Salt . .	6,32,97	6,69,81	6,63,18	7,59,93	6,76,46
Land revenue	35,55,31	34,88,31	35,68,73	33,16,21	33,47,11
Excise .	19,89,87	19,82,68	19,82,16	19,97,70	20,41,23
Stamps .	13,65,60	13,19,62	13,57,90	13,73,05	14,12,42
Registration	1,45,38	1,45,70	1,47,33	1,43,40	1,37,03
Schedules Taxes .	35,12	36,46	40,66	43,08	40,55
Net Profit from Rlys.	5,51,23	6,02,30	6,31,93	5,25,39	6,14,18
Irrigation .	2,39,04	1,64,77	1,50,10	2,05,45	1,88,20
Total .	149,04,51	147,46,05	149,06,05	149,97,87	152,91,19

Annual average for the Quinquennium 1925-26 to 1929-30 = Rs. 149,69,13,000 or Rs. 149·7 crores.

income. In calculating the totals of taxation, we have not taken into account the revenue from forests and opium; opium was a State monopoly the incidence of whose tax-element fell on foreigners, while forests are a property of the State revenue from which is really in the nature of fees and return for sale of produce. In the case of railways and irrigation, we have taken into account only the net figure, i.e. the profits remaining after meeting working expenses and interest on debt. We have not taken into account the net revenue from post and telegraphs department, as the net profit of the first two years of our quinquennium is offset by a corresponding loss in the last two years. The detailed figures are in Table 79, on p. 159.

The results of our inquiry into the burden of taxation are as follows :—

National Dividend	Rs. 20230 millions
Taxation (central and provincial)	Rs. 1497 millions
Taxation per head	Rs. 5-12-1
Proportion of taxation per head to national income per head	7·4 per cent.

This percentage may be compared with those for a number of other countries :—[1]

Great Britain	18·4
Canada	13·6
Australia	15·7
The United States	5·7
France	14·2
Italy	5·8

[1] Taken from Table XXII, Appendix—Shirras' "The Science of Public Finance."

It is true that the percentage of the Indian's income taken by his State is smaller than that taken from the nationals of the countries mentioned above by their respective States. But the comparatively heavier burden of Indian taxation becomes clear when we take into account the following factors :—

(1) The figures given for Great Britain, France, etc., refer to an immediate post-war year, since when taxation has been appreciably reduced in those countries so that if figures were available for the period, 1925-29, the percentages would be much lower.

(2) The tax revenues raised in India are not all spent in India, nor are they spent on Indian nationals only, so that at least part of the taxes raised operates as a *real* deduction and not as a mere transfer expenditure as in the case of other countries.

(3) It is a well-known fact, that a rupee taken from an income of Rs. 100 inflicts a much heavier loss than one taken from an income of Rs. 1000; what is true of individuals in this case is much more true of nations, for countries whose income is just sufficient to meet their minimum needs of subsistence have really no taxable capacity. In the case of all the countries mentioned above, their *per capita* income is very much larger, and the real burden of taxation per a given percentage is correspondingly lower.

There is no doubt that the burden of taxation is quite heavy in India; this, however, should not be taken to imply on our part a plea for reduction in taxation. We are one of those who believe that the burden of taxation is really determined by the direction and objects of public expenditure, and taxable capacity can itself be increased by a judicious and planned policy relating to public expenditure. But this is not the proper place to enter into discussions relating to the theory of public finance.

Conclusion.

We conclude this essay with a feeling of sadness. Our investigations have revealed a profoundly disquieting state of economic affairs in India. Our income is low, and though we are moving forward, our pace is that of a snail. In the meanwhile, our population continues to expand, and our potentialities of production still await exploitation. What we really need is a careful and well thought out planning of our economic life. If our productive powers are not to remain for ever a latent asset, we must have rapid, organised and extensive development of our capital resources; and public expenditure on capital works must increase to a point much beyond that contemplated by the cautious imagination of those at present in power.[1] Planning necessarily implies initiative on the part of the State. Discussions of this and other

[1] This was written in February 1935. Since then, of course, a change for the better has taken place in the composition of the provincial governments. But even in their case it is true to say that problems of distribution are commanding their attention more than those of production.

details of planning, however, will again take us outside the scope of this essay and had, therefore, be postponed to another volume. But the conclusion of our essay remains that the national income is so low that radical measures are necessary and can be permitted for increasing it.

APPENDIX

APPENDIX TO CHAPTER I: "PREVIOUS ESTIMATES"

Dr. Dadabhai Naoroji.

	(Crores of Rs.)
Value of agricultural produce . . .	260
,, meat, milk, fish	15
,, produce of industry . . .	15
,, mines and commerce . . .	17
Contingencies	33
Total . . .	340

Population	170 millions.
Per capita income	Rs. 20

Baring-Barbour.

	(Crores of Rs.)
Agricultural income .	350
Non-agricultural income	175
Total income .	525

Population .	195 millions
Per capita income	Rs. 27

Made up as under:

	(Lakhs of Rs.)
Punjab . .	3,415
N.W. provinces and Oudh .	7,175
Bengal . .	10,350
C.P. . . .	2,125
Bombay . .	3,900
Madras . .	5,000
Add for rest of India, Burma and Assam	3,035
	35,000

(Quoted from Digby, pp. 364-365.)

Digby[1] ("Prosperous British India," p. 611).

Province.	Agricultural income.	Non-agricultural income.	Total.	*Per capita* income in Rs.
	(Figures in thousands of £)			Rs. as. ps.
Bengal . .	53,930	21,702	75,632	15 3 0
Madras . .	20,323	15,650	35,973	14 2 0
Bombay . .	16,211	20,066	36,277	29 1 0
N.W. Provinces and Oudh .	44,243	12,275	56,523	18 2 6
Punjab . .	11,973	6,899	18,872	12 10 0
C. P. . .	8,465	3,003	11,468	16 12 0
Burmah, Upper and Lower .	11,471	4,260	15,731	22 12 0
Assam	8,197	1,059	9,256	25 8 9
		Total	259,732	

Atkinson.

SECTION I. AGRICULTURE

(Figures in thousands)

Description.	Production.		Price per cwt.		Value of production.	
	1875.	1895.	1875.	1895.	1875.	1895.
Food Crops .	1,064,535	1,298,134	2·7	3·5	291,64,03	458,57,33
Non-food Crops	70,429	101,452	6·7	7·7	47,41,04	78,69,33
Grand Total (including other crops) . .					351,58,65	558,76,44

[1] Ajemere-Merwara and other minor states under the direct government of the Indian Foreign Office are omitted in the above summary, the details not being available. They, however, if included, would not appreciably affect the results arrived at.

Atkinson.

SECTION II. NON-AGRICULTURE

(In thousands)

Head.	1875.		1895.	
	Population.	Income Rs.	Population.	Income Rs.
Labourers	16,310	31,49,66	18,870	41,62,88
Domestic	7,011	19,79,64	8,626	30,59,76
Industrial	29,805	105,83,63	35,180	150,43,64
Military	414	44,00,93	450	5,08,21
Administration	3,123	11,13,26	3,779	14,62,38
Commerce	611	4,44,99	748	6,26,10
Transport	2,588	6,32,20	3,253	10,68,55
Miscellaneous	5,198	17,34,92	6,028	22,40,16
Total	65,060	200,39,32	76,934	281,71,69

SECTION III. CLASSES OF AMPLE OR SUFFICIENT MEANS

	1895. (In thousands of Rs.)
Professions	22,88,80
Commerce	52,05,00
Civil and military officers	8,10,00
Agents, managers, etc.	20,64,00
Private incomes	10,72,20
Total	114,40,00

Sir B. N. Sarma.

Statement made in the Council of State, June 1921. *Per capita* income, Rs. 50 in 1911.

Findlay Shirras.[1]

AGRICULTURAL INCOME OF BRITISH INDIA, 1920-21, 1921-22

(In thousands)

Description.	Area.		Value.	
	1920-21.	1921-22.	1920-21.	1921-22.
Total food crops	199,245	217,755	1054,52,00	1367,86,00
Total fibres	17,316	13,869	61,34,00	53,95,00
Total oilseeds	26,485	25,862	77,34,00	77,42,00
Total dyes	729	854	7,79,00	9,46,00
Rubber	75	76	73,00	29,00
Miscellaneous, non-food	1,089	942	5,45,00	4,71,00
Straw	133,180	142,219	79,32,00	101,30,00
Fodder	8,108	8,593	34,77,00	42,97,00
Milk	—	—	278,75,00	310,36,00
Wool	—	—	1,24,00	1,23,00
Hides	—	—	6,55,00	7,46,00
Forest Produce	—	—	6,22,00	6,40,00
Grand Total	238,933	256,285	1714,94,00	1983,41,00

[1] "The Science of Public Finance," pp.139-140. The whole discussion is to be found in pp. 138-149.

Shah and Khambhata.[1]

ANNUAL WEALTH OF INDIA

Items.	Pre-war period 1900-14.	War and post-war period 1914-22.	Whole period 1900-22.	Year 1921-22.
	(Figures in Crores of Rs.)			
Total food crops . .	793·4	1306·0	978·3	1768·5
Total oilseeds . .	55·5	82·6	65·7	105·6
Total fibres . .	81·2	129·2	100·6	107·3
Total dyes . . .	2·4	5·1	3·4	4·6
Opium . . .	9·3	4·8	8·6	4·6
Tea	10·5	17·5	12·3	15·4
Coffee . . .	1·8	1·9	1·8	2·0
Tobacco . . .	12·0	18·0	14·4	20·4
Other drugs and narcotics . . .	·7	1·4	1·0	1·4
Fodder crops . .	48·0	114·0	72·0	126·0
Total agricultural produce . . .	1014·8	1686·5	1257·1	2155·8
Deduct for seeds . .	— 20	— 35	— 25	— 58
Net agricultural production . . .	994·8	1651·5	1232·1	2097·8
Income from cattle .	Nil (see footnote to table)[2]			
Total forest wealth .	10·0	20·0	14·0	28·0
Fisheries . . .	1·2	2·5	1·9	3·2
Total manufactures .	80·0	150·0	106·0	186·0
Total mineral wealth .	10·0	21·6	14·0	28·7
Building, etc. . .	10·0	16·4	12·0	20·3
Grand Total	1106·0	1862·0	1380·0	2364·0

[1] *Loc. cit.*, pp. 199-200.

[2] "Values of hides, and skins, bones, horns, manure, meat, milk, accretions to livestock, etc., are taken to be set off by the cost of upkeep of animals, so as to leave income *nil*."

Wadia and Joshi, 1913-14.

Item.	Value of output.	Remarks.
	(Figures in Lakhs of Rs.)	
Food crops	847,78	
Total oilseeds . . .	43,71	
Total fibres . . .	139,96	
Indigo	56	
Opium	3,16	
Coffee	1,32	
Tea	6,56	
Tobacco	21,92	
Fodder crops . . .	4,93	
Other non-food crops . .	3,10	
Total agricultural production	1,073,00	
Deduct 20 per cent. . .	214,60	for seed, wastage, etc.
Net agricultural production .	858,40	
Net mineral production .	11,53	After deducting 20 per cent.
Hides and skins . . .	4,00	Assuming that exports constitute 80 per cent. of the total production.
Manures	1,18	,, ,, ,,
Wool	3,11	,, ,, ,,
Silk	31	,, ,, ,,
Poultry products . .	25	,, ,, ,,
Fisheries	5,95	At 4 annas per head for 275 days for 865,000 persons.
Valuation of products worked by artisans, and earnings of labourers engaged in trade and transport . .	139,50	At 4 annas per head per day for 310 days for 18,000,000 persons.
Net valuation of the produce of livestock . . .	145,10	
Net valuation of manufactures	40,95	At 20 per cent of the gross total of raw material.
Grand Total	1,210,28	

Vakil and Muranjan.

GROSS TOTAL PRODUCTION OF INDIA, 1911-14

	(In Crores of Rs.)	
Food stuffs	840·6	
Raw materials	216·1	
Condiments, etc.	38·5	
Other fibres	13·0	
Minerals	13·3	
Cattle	606·4	
Forest	10·2	
Industries	36·0	
Total gross income	1774·3	
Total population in millions		315·0
Minus population supported by handicrafts, exclusive of handloom workers, in millions		11·8
		303·2
Per head gross income in Rs.		58·5

(P. 394, "Currency and Prices in India.")

INDEX

For Product Safety Concerns and Information please contact our EU representative GPSR@taylorandfrancis.com Taylor & Francis Verlag GmbH, Kaufingerstraße 24, 80331 München, Germany